Indian Garden Flowers

Home Gardener's Guide

*An Amateur Gardener's Handbook
for identification, propagation and care of garden flowers*

Amarjeet Singh Batth

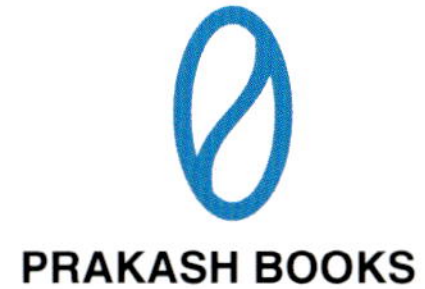

PRAKASH BOOKS

Published 2007 by
Prakash Books India Pvt. Ltd.
1, Ansari Road, Daryaganj,
New Delhi 110 002, India
sales@prakashbooks.com,
www.prakashbooks.com
Tel.: 011-23247062-65

Text and Photographs: Amarjeet Singh Batth

ISBN: 978-81-7234-144-2

Printed & bound in India at
Rave India, New Delhi

A tribute to a soldier, my father,
Major Jagir Singh 'Kokri'
Vir-Chakra & Mention-in-Despatch (J&K, 1948)
7th Battalion (now 5th Battalion),
The Sikh Regiment

Contents

Acknowledgements

At the onset I wish to extend my sincere gratitude to Dr. Ajai Pal Singh Gill, Ph.D formerly Professor of Floriculture, PAU, Ludhiana, National Consultant Floriculture UNDP & FAO projects for his guidance and encouragement throughout the making of this book.

Further, I shall forever remain indebted to my mother for her moral support who passed away during the conceptualization of the book. Her love and blessings have made this book see the light of the day.

Mr. Naresh Bedi and Mr. Rajesh Bedi deserve special mention for their motivation and help.

My thanks are also due to Dr. G.S. Dhaliwal, Ph.D, formerly Professor of Ecology, PAU, Ludhiana, Dr. Neelam Mehrotra and Dr. Pushpinder Kaur Sandhu, both from the Dept. of Family Resource Management, PAU, Ludhiana.

Thanks to all who have helped and supported me.

Foreword

We often get fascinated watching elegant flowers but are seldom able to grow them with desired results. There was a need for an interactive, illustrative, compact manual for the layman.

Growing seasonal flowers requires an artistic approach. The brief, objective layout information given in this manual will help a gardener match the various colour combinations, hues and spread of the flowering plants to give a uniform effect to the garden. Barring a few flowers, a common man has limited knowledge about their identity, method of propagation and post-planting care. He uses set cultivation practices which do not yield quality bloom. This handbook presents in tabular form select propagation information for easy assimilation. Illustrations of flowers along with seeds and flower beds leave nothing to the imagination and give an almost practical look to the whole concept. The tastefully selected couplets glorify the significance of flowers making this manual more absorbing.

It is indeed interesting to note that a defence officer with admiration for flowers has combined his photographic creativity to present an illustrative and interactive manual on seasonal flowers grown in the sub-tropical plains of northern India. His creativity in using planting materials is well reflected in his own garden where he has experimented with growing numerous kinds of flowers in different hues and fragrances. He has been passionately involved in compiling his maiden work which is admirable. He has come forward to share his experience in gardening in this manual which shall prove to be much beneficial for garden lovers.

Avtar Singh Dhindsa
Member, Board of Management,
Punjab Agricultural University, Ludhiana
Member, Farmer Commission, Punjab

List of Flowers

Introduction

*"In the hope of reaching the moon,
man failed to see the flowers that blossom at their feet."*
Albert Schweitzer

To have beautiful flowers around is anyone's delight but to establish a garden, one needs to be in love with the plants and should have the sensitivity towards flora. Those who really love flowers are never indifferent to them. A gardener needs to understand the language of flora and converse with them. Gardening is not only getting work done from hired labour but the care and concern you show for the plants. Plants too breathe; they need water, food and care from the extremities of climate. Plants are not demanding and possess lots of tolerance; they bear with whatever they can and then perish in silence giving a deserted look to your so-called garden. Plants do not fail; instead, we make them fail by not rendering proper care. Spare a few moments for your garden; consider it a part of your family and nurture it. Watch the plants growing, see the beautiful flowers, enjoy the changing colours, feel their fragrance, cherish the bloom, appreciate their shapes and sure enough you will derive the same warmth and pleasure as you get from your family.

Gardening, today, is getting relegated more to become one's hobby than a thing of passion. However, it can bring about pleasing changes in a person's life. The garden of a house offers a place for relaxation, contentment and positive energy; it relieves one of mental stress and routines of a hectic life. It always has a welcoming effect, making the home dearer and a place to look forward to. In fact, a good garden not only gives the owner pride and satisfaction but also praise and emotional upliftment from others. A nicely designed garden speaks volumes of the creativity and taste of the person who has maintained it.

This manual facilitates identification of flowers and furnishes information about growing seasonal flowers. It caters to the two major problems faced by an amateur gardener while propagating seasonal flowers. First, the difficulty in memorizing their identity as the flowers being seasonal are short-lived. Secondly, lack of cultivation knowledge that creates dependence on the shallow awareness of the local 'Mali'. What an amateur gardener needs is brief cultivation information coupled with a few tips that he can adopt and not exhaustive details which may become dull and time-consuming. The contents of this manual will also build confidence to design your own garden. The subject-matter is concise, time-saving and can be glanced at convenience without going into commercial, theoretical and technical details.

The principles of planning a home garden are highlighted in the beginning for easy absorption and implementation. Irrespective of the area available, one may understand the essence of gardening and use of one's creativity. It is not mandatory to incorporate all the features discussed to make the garden look beautiful but judiciously consider which are relevant in the context of the garden. To add colour to your garden it is essential to allocate a place for seasonal flowers during the designing stage.

The core component of this book is the illustrations of seasonal flowers. The emphasis is on making them see as they look in the garden, close to the real. Thereafter, you may consider their growth potential, colour patterns and accordingly select them for your garden. The photo plate is supplemented with cultivation details in a tabular form for easy understanding. This information pertains to the genus of flower and does not represent the coverage of the entire species, which have a large range of colours, foliage, size and characteristics. For layman understanding, the botanical name has two components: the first word denotes the 'genus' and its first letter is written in the capital form. The second word represents the 'species' and its first letter is written in small. The third component is not commonly used which stands for variety and is represented by 'var'. There are also new hybrids being developed by cross-pollination which are known by different names.

In the subsequent chapter, cultivation details pertaining to seasonal flowers are discussed. Once the seeds sprout into saplings they need care for their growth, which involves regular monitoring of gardening activities. Special care needs to be taken for the flowering plants during their bloom. Manures and fertilizers are important because they supplement the soil nutrients.

Owing to the vast geographical area of India and variation in climatic conditions no standard time-plan can be laid out for sowing of the flowers. The time-plan suggested in this manual is for the north-west plains of India having sub-topical climates. In the north-western plains, annuals are classified into the following categories: summer, rainy, and winter blooming flowers. However, in the temprate climate of the highlands of Himalayas in North India the nursery of seasonal flower is raised during August-September. In South India where the climate remains moderate throughout the year with no distinct winter, summer and rainy season, all flowers, except a few, grow well and are sown in March-April. Time variations for different locations may be made in consultation with state agricultural institutions.

Flowers are cultivated to adorn gardens and also indoors where they are used as cut flowers and dried flowers. The arrangement of fresh and dry flowers looks elegant and find place indoors. Dried flowers embellish your dwelling even for a reasonably long period and can be carried away from their natural habitat to far-off places. This manual will only acquaint the reader about the usage of cut and dried flowers and these floral designs will inspire you to know more about this art.

These days various disease-resistant varieties and hybrids are being developed yet diseases, insects and pests attack the plants. The tips on symptomatic diagnosis and control measures for healthy bloom are also given in a tabular form. Finally, a checklist has been prepared to remind of round-the-year cultivation activities and after-care of plants.

There is also an exhaustive study material available on the subject. To have specific information and details refer to any floriculture institution or alternatively visit a nearby library.

Design your Home Garden

The trouble with gardening is that it does not remain an avocation
*It becomes an obsession... **Phyllis McGinley***

Floral ambience is God's greatest gift to mankind. Since times immemorial, man has endeavoured to relish the beauty and serenity of flora bestowed upon him by the Almighty. Modernization and mechanization may have curtailed the size of the home garden and put man in the time race but not curbed his zest to be around natural surroundings. To enjoy the gifts of nature in their natural setting and to make up for this void man tries to create around himself a microcosm of the earth's floral legacy popularly known as 'The Garden'. A garden presents a combination of trees, shrubs, climbers, perennials and annual flowers, which are arranged according to their size, area under foliage, colour, soil texture, drainage and sunlight requirements. The scope and form of a garden may vary tremendously according to land size, differences in taste and budget.

Plants lend serenity to the surroundings and make the environment clean and peaceful. A garden is designed not only for beauty but also for utility. In ancient times in India a garden was an enclosed place, walled or fenced in the vicinity of a temple. Apart from having ornamental plantation it had an earmarked location for orchard and a place for planting herbs used for medicinal purposes. Hymns in the *Vedas* and the poetry of Kalidas mention the components and essence of 'vatika' of Indian culture.

A garden of today is quite different in comparison to the one in ancient days. Today, while planning a home garden one has to strike a fine balance between beauty and utility. The beauty pertains to outlook, attraction and pleasantness and forms the formal area, while utility is in terms of productivity which is catered in informal area. Formal area is the area along the front wall, entrance, drive-in area, and front lawn while informal area refers to the kitchen-garden, orchard yard, waste disposal area and playing area. The informal area can be screened from the formal area using hedges, shrubs and climbers. The garden may be informal or formless; the unity or balance is achieved by asymmetrical planning. The feature may not be architectural and the curves may not be used to simulate naturalness or informality. The formal types of gardens with straight lines define the boundaries and are easy to plan.

Knowledge of plant material is not enough to design a garden. The sense of interpreting the design is equally important. The priority of one person may not be the area of concern for the other. Different likings, needs and requirements of people at home should not be ignored while planning the garden. However, thorough planning also may not attain the desired shape and size due to a lot of factors. Therefore, the setting can be changed in

"

coming years by replacing the plants that have not grown to give the desired effect. This change should be done in a phased manner so that the garden does not wear a shabby look. Also, try new plants as and when deemed fit. Never think that you have achieved perfection as there is always scope for improvement with the passage of time. A garden cannot be made perfect in one day but it can be enriched day by day, year by year.

Planning Considerations

A home garden is developed differently by different people. The following points have to be considered while setting a new garden or renovating an existing garden. These points are very basic and can be implemented conveniently but professional help within reasonable financial limits is always better to novice effort.

▶ The garden is carved out from the plot available. Drawing a rough sketch of the garden area along with existing structures on a piece of paper is the first step towards planning a garden. This exercise utilizes most of the land available. One must bear in mind that a garden must be planned 'on site' and never indoors. This helps in selecting the right plants considering their growth potential and the visible effect they will create at every angle of the garden, from inside and outside the house. Look for the view you get from windows and doors of your garden sitting inside the house.

▶ The shape and dimension of the garden is of importance while planning large-size commercial gardens, which require meticulous planning. Planning a home garden is, however, relatively free from such elaborate details. But this does not mean that a home garden can be set up in an arbitrary fashion. The fundamental principle of gardening cannot be ignored to achieve an optimal turnout. On the other hand, people living in flats and apartments have a limited space or no space and the only option available is to grow pot plants, baskets and windows boxes.

▶ A good gradient is essential as it will ensure proper drainage, which is the pre-requisite for most of the plants. Location of water source and its availability is also of prime consideration. Plants are also propagated depending upon the quantum and frequency of their water requirement.

▶ The requirements of all plants cannot be standardized in the garden. Segmentise the garden according to the requirements of each plant, i.e., kind of soil, sunlight, drainage and water consumption. Plants should be sown according to the texture of the soil available. Alternatively, prepare the soil beds according to the needs of the chosen plant.

▶ Identify a focal area in the garden. It is the place of highest design centre with most striking plants which are maintained with the highest degree of upkeep. The garden should have some unique plants different from others as ordinary plants draw neither the visitors nor the gardener. Keep in mind to select those plants which are suitable to local climatic conditions else they will not grow to give desired results. The adventure of exploring something new, different and less popular yet unique will give your garden an impressive look.

◗ Mark the position of each plant on the rough sketch, evaluate the position in relation to that of the other plants and take the final decision only after fully convincing yourself of its sound placement. It is useful effort to mark the position so that required adjustments can be made later on the spot.

◗ The most important factor is the orientation of the sun and the actual amount of sunlight available during the day, during different seasons. On an average, a plant requires five to six hours of direct sunlight in a day. Prefer planting deciduous trees in the eastern and southern side so that they let maximum sunlight during winters and provide shade during summers. The flower beds should be made away from the 'drip line' of the trees and big shrubs, as they will deprive the plants not only of sunlight but of nutrients also. A south- and west-backed wall give more heat and light to flowers in comparison to north- and east-backed walls or fence.

The structures of the house and surrounding buildings, the existing plantations inside and outside the house influence the layout of the garden and the selection of plants. If the existing surrounding plantations are impressive, blend and exploit them to your advantage.

◗ Choose suitable plants for an appropriate place keeping in mind the above factors. However, if the basic factors are not considered the plants will not be healthy and will lose their original size and shape. The garden will bear an unattractive look and not yield the desired effect.

Indeed, seasonal flowers provide the real boost to the garden and add colour to it. Flowering plants are short-lived and are followed by gaps between next phases of bloom. The trees and the shrubs fill the gap by their glorious display, thus maintaining the charm of the garden. While choosing seasonal flowers the best and the most practical approach is to identify flowers of your choice and then select those that can flourish in your garden. Thereafter, propagate either the same flowering plants on yearly rotation basis or you may propagate them as standard plantation without any change. Finally, the choice of plant varies from person to person and the understanding of their behaviour comes with experience.

As a basic principal, permanent trees and shrubs should form the background of the garden. In cities where space is restricted the surrounding trees on public land can be used to form the background of your home garden. Generally, plants are planted in the descending order of their height, tall at the rear side, medium in the middle and small in the front side.

◗ Other factors – the garden should give a spacious look, i.e., appear bigger than actual and not cramped with plantation. If the garden looks dark during the night it signifies that it is crowded. It should not hide the house but should blend with it and invite attention with its beauty and grace. Plants should not be arranged in a manner that make them lose their glamour by inter-mingling of species with each other but must merge harmoniously. Whenever any bifurcation, partition or screening is done take care that the continuity is not broken and harmony is retained. A fine blending is the real beauty of the garden.

A garden is incomplete without hedges and borders.

Shape it with a tasteful range of varieties as per the requirement, especially if it is to be used for creating micro-regions, boundary, for privacy, as a windbreak or to separate informal area from formal area. A well chosen, compact and nicely trimmed hedge gives neat and tidy look to the garden. The best time for propagation is February-March or during the monsoon season. Dig a trench 30 cm x 30 cm and expose the soil to sun for 2-3 weeks. Add well rotten farmyard manure to enrich the dug-up soil. A dose of anti-termite is compulsory in the effected area. Firmly settle and level the soil as undulating ground will result in unequal growth levels. A space of 4-6 cm must be left for watering. Hedges can be planted in single/double row depending on how compact the growth is required. Distance from one plant to another could be 8-12 inches and one row to another 6-8 inches. All the hedges must be trimmed regularly, especially during the early growth period to encourage compact growth. Hedges are also made from shrubs and trees.

Climbers are used to cover or camouflage a place and sometimes serve to highlight the contours of the building. They require same care as required by the other plants. Climbers have a natural tendency to grow straight causing the main shoot to get exposed. When it is trained straight its falling branches cover the main shoot but when trained in horizontal position the main stem gets invisible.

Identify plants and places for pots as they form an important component of the garden. A separate location for developing pots in an enclosed area to maintain supply chain of seasonal flowers in the garden is essential.

Last but not the least is the cost factor. The garden can bear a slash in the budget but will not compromise on any cut in terms of time and labour.

Gardeners should take caution and take up light warming-up exercises prior to getting involved in the various tasks of gardening to avoid backache, pulling of muscles and ligament-related problems.

Position of the Seasonal Flowers

Flowers are the first love of every human being. Apart from the beauty and aesthetic value of flowers, they are used to convey the inner feeling of a person. They have found a definite purpose in human lives encircling religious, social and adornment purposes.

The seasonal flowers are spaced between the trees, shrubs and lawn. They fill the void, create a balance, unity and proportion in the garden. Seasonal flowers should be avoided growing against walls but should be planted with a herbaceous background. They are planted in beds, along the borders, along pavements, etc. The seasonal flowers in Indian plains are divided into three categories such as summer, rainy and winter blooming flowers.

Seeds for summer flowers are sown in the month of February-March and are transplanted in March-April in North India. The rainy blooming seeds are sown in May-June and transplanted with the outbreak of early monsoons in July-August. The majority of the flowers which bloom during spring season are sown in September-October and are transplanted between September-November. The bonanza is short-lived but the impression of its glorious display is memorable.

While planting the seasonal flowers as herbaceous borders with the tall ones at far end, medium size in the middle and small at near end, ensure that the blooming duration of all these plants should be the same else the short-blooming flowers will form dry patches giving an ugly look to the plantation in the garden.

Earmark space exclusive for cut flowers if you are keen to have flower arrangement as this will cater to the need of cut flowers for home use.

Plan the garden in such a way that there is life and movement throughout the year, keeping you involved and generating curiosity. A seasoned gardener uses his experience and imagination to develop different colour combinations through contrast, shade and tones of the flowers. Plants also change colours with change of weather – the spring is full of colours and fresh leaves, winter experiences shedding of leaves giving a dull look and monotonous feeling. He can also grow flowers of single colour in beds of various sizes to have a mass effect. Knowledge of the basic colours (red, green, yellow), cool colours (violet, blue, green), warm colours (yellow, orange, red), and neutral colours (black, white and its combinations) is very essential. A variety of species are available in varying height and hue to give a gorgeously colourful look to the garden.

Terrace Garden

A terrace garden can be developed if there is no ground space available or in addition to it. It requires more care and is a bit expensive but worth the ambience it generates. The main area of concern is to ensure if the roofs have the strength to take the additional load of the plantation. Secondly, be careful for proper drainage. Thirdly, grow plants which require less water and have fibrous root system to avoid any damage to the structure of the house. The roof should be given waterproofing treatment before developing a garden on it. An expert guidance is a must for developing terrace garden.

Creativity

Creativity of the gardener needs no rules but is only an understanding of the essence of gardening. The limitations of the ground, viz., an old well, a nearby drain, a rock boulder or an undulated surface, etc. should be used to its advantage. Water effects are formed by making waterfall or fountain which must blend with the garden design. Lighting using pole lights, pathway lights, landscape bollards, landscape spots, flower bed lights, wall-mounting brackets and lanterns enhance the beauty of the garden during night. If space allows add artistic structures, erect arches, make pathways inside the garden, form steps to cover up the gradients and have nice sitting arrangements to improve the aesthetic appeal of the garden. A corner bar to enjoy drink, wind chimes to listen to the music of the gentle breeze and a swing to feel the cool wind are some additional attractions which can enhance the beauty of the garden.

Common Garden Features

There are some common features seen in the gardens which can be used in your design.

▶ If the garden is big in size, develop pavements.

▶ A wall can be covered with a beautiful climber.

▶ Develop variation in altitude to provide diversity of landscape.

▶ The entrance should have an attractive and open look to it.

▶ Trees act as excellent wind barrier and form a beautiful skyline.

▶ The flower beds can be planned with the lawn in the foreground.

▶ Climbers, shrubs and flowering plants can be added for fragrance.

▶ A kitchen and fruit garden can be isolated with screening or partition effect.

▶ The garden grows more fascinating if a corner or a concealed point is developed.

▶ Encourage birds to make their nest in the trees; let a small place be made available for the birds to drink water.

▶ A pond with water plants adds another dimension and makes the garden interesting.

Points to Ponder

- Develop an easy-to-maintain garden.
- Make a home garden, not a botanical garden.
- Fresh air, adequate sunlight, water and manure are essential to all plants.
- Excessive water, fertilizers and extreme temperature conditions are harmful to plants.
- Do not overcrowd or flood your garden with multiple colour plants.
- Make a mention of your choice to the supplier before buying seeds or seedlings from the nursery.
- Irrespective of the type of grass if there are weeds, brown patches and the grass is not mowed, it will give an ugly look.
- Too much symmetry in the home garden is not advisable because if some plants happen to perish the gap caused will give an ugly look.
- The older the plants, the more aesthetic value they add to the garden.
- It is worthwhile to share the experiences and take advice from fellow gardeners.
- Cherish the plantation sown by others and add some for others to enjoy.
- Develop a habit of reading books on floriculture.
- Visit flower shows and floriculture institutions occasionally.

Selecting the Annuals

What do these mean?

Botanical Name : Genus and species

Family : Botanical identification (morphological resemblance)

Common Name : Local name

Raising of Seedling : The time period when seeds are sown in the flower bed or in nursery bed

Transplanting Month : The time period when seedlings are transferred into the flower bed

Planting Distance : Row to row, plant to plant

Height of the Plant : Dwarf: up to 30 cm
Medium: 30-60 cm
Tall: 60 cm & above

Flowering Month : Blooming period, flowering duration, duration from beginning to the end of flowering

Colours : Range of colours

Soil : Light/Sandy: grains which are felt by hand
Medium/Loamy: texture of soil in-between
Heavy/Clayey: soils that stick to hand

Sunlight : Full: 8-10 hrs of sunlight, Partial: Sunlight in the morning and in the evening & shade during noon for less than 4 hours or diffused sunlight under shade or cover

Irrigation : Mild: Once in week
Normal: Twice a week
Heavy: Alternate day

Suitable For : Any location in the garden where the flowers will flourish and give the best effect in consideration to their morphology

Points to Remember

* All seasonal flowers generally require a rich, well-drained soil and an open sunny spot.

* All plants prefer morning light as photosynthesis is maximum up to noon.

* Shady annual plants do survive in full sunlight while plants that require full sunlight, do not flourish in shade.

* Heavy irrigation is required for all summer flowers while a mild dose is sufficient for rainy season flowers.

* The time and period of nursery raising and planting of seasonal flowers varies with the climatic conditions of the region.

Paper Flower

Botanical Name	:	*Acroclinum roseum*
Family	:	Compositae
Common Name	:	Paper Flower/Everlasting Flower
Raising of Seedling	:	September-October
Transplanting Month	:	October-November
Planting Distance	:	30 cm x 30 cm
Height of Plant	:	Tall: 60-75 cm
Flowering Month	:	February-March
Colours	:	Pink and white with bright golden-yellow dark centre
Soil	:	Light
Sunlight	:	Full
Irrigation	:	Moderate
Suitable For	:	Bedding, dry flowers and as cut flowers

Flowers may beckon us,
but they speak toward heaven and God.
Henry Ward Beecher

Acroclinum roseum is a hardy annual with narrow smooth leaves. The single flowers are daisy-like, papery in texture and appear at the end of each stem.

Seeds take 6 to 8 weeks for seedling formation. However, direct sowing can also be done which are later thinned. The plant is free-flowering and flowers appear quite early within 40-50 days of sowing. In the northern hills, sowing is done from March to April. Dry conditions are more suitable than humid climate.

Flowers retain their form, colour and papery texture for a long time even on drying, therefore, they are best suitable for dry decoration. While using as a dried flower, take a fully opened flower and then dry using air-drying method. Insert a thin wire in the stem to keep it straight and erect.

Holly Hock

Botanical Name	:	*Althaea rosea*
Family	:	Malvaceae
Common Name	:	Holly Hock
Raising of Seedling	:	August-September
Transplanting Month	:	September-October
Planting Distance	:	45 cm x 45 cm
Height of Plant	:	Tall: 150-180 cm
Flowering Month	:	March-April
Colours	:	White, pink, yellow, mauve, deep violet
Soil	:	Heavy
Sunlight	:	Full
Irrigation	:	Normal
Suitable For	:	Screening; background and back row of a herbaceous border

Flowers are the sweetest things
God ever made, and forgot to put a soul into.
Henry Ward Beecher – *Life Thoughts*

The stem is erect, cylindrical, branched, hairy, solid and green. The leaves are petiolate, alternate, palmately, lobed, rough and kidney-shaped. The inflorescence is solitary axillary or in axillary cymose clusters. Holly Hock is borne on long spikes and grows 8-10 cm in size. The thin petals are fragile and crumble in short time once the flower is detached from the stem.

The disc-shaped seeds are generally sown directly and later thinning is done for equal coverage. Seldom seeds are sown for seedling as injury to its root system retards its growth. *Althaea rosea* is a tall plant which shows vigorous growth. A good spacing yields better results. It has a well-developed tap root system which requires well-dug and rich soil. The roots do not enjoy disturbance, therefore add adequate quantity of manure while sowing. It takes more than four months to bloom. Therefore, the seeds are sown a month earlier than the other annuals for a combined bloom effect with other winter flowers. Late bloom does not give an impressive and rich colourful splendour. The new varieties bear double-flower leaf, which makes the flower look more elegant.

Fungal diseases also affect the bloom once the plant is fully established. It is sown for its tall height, large-sized flower and longer duration of bloom till May.

Bikni

Botanical Name	:	*Amobium alatum*
Family	:	Compositae
Common Name	:	Bikni
Raising of Seedling	:	November
Transplanting Month	:	October-November
Planting Distance	:	15 cm x 15 cm
Height of Plant	:	60 cm
Flowering Month	:	February-April
Colours	:	White petals with prominent yellow centre
Soil	:	Medium
Sunlight	:	Full
Irrigation	:	Normal
Suitable For	:	Beddings, as cut flowers and dry flowers

The seeds are transplanted and can be sown directly. Later thinning is done. The flowers are coat button shaped. They are excellent fillers in bouquets and in floral designs. They are more commonly used as dry flowers. The flowers are picked up when two-third open and then air-dried. Artificial dye can also be used to get the desired colour of flower.

Dog Flower

Botanical Name	:	*Antirrhinum majus*
Family	:	Scrophulariaceae
Common Name	:	Dog Flower/Snapdragon
Raising of Seedling	:	September-October
Transplanting Month	:	October-November
Planting Distance	:	45 cm x 30 cm
Height of Plant	:	Medium: 45-60 cm to Tall: 60-90 cm
Flowering Month	:	February-April
Colours	:	Crimson, yellow, fawn, purple, scarlet, pink, white and mixed colours
Soil	:	Heavy
Sunlight	:	Full
Irrigation	:	Mild
Suitable For	:	Borders, beddings, edging, backgrounds, rock gardens, and as pot and cut flowers

The plant is sturdy and the leaves are simple, thin, smooth and narrow. The upper leaves are alternate while the lower ones are pods opposite. The long spikes bear flowers in row which are tubular in form and have two conspicuous curiously shaped tips at the top.

Antirrhinum majus is a perennial but treated as annual for better results. The minute seeds are sown in nursery beds and later transplanted. The height of the plants ranges from dwarf, medium and tall varieties. However, there are few spreading varieties as well. The size of the flower may vary according to the variety. The plant survives ideally in a well-drained soil and under dry conditions. Pinching is done when the plant is 15 cm in height which increases the number of flower but reduces the size. Excess manure contributes more towards the foliage growth. In March a top dressing of a teaspoon of ammonium sulphate and sulphates of potash is good for the bloom. It takes about 90-120 days for the flower to appear. In hills, they are sown in February-March and August-September.

The beautiful flowers of *Antirrhinum majus* form an impressive fresh flower arrangement. It is cut when the flower is one-third open and has a cut life of 6-7 days. Its artistic shape and size makes it suitable for all styles of floral designs. However, they are used as 'fillers' in large arrangements. The stems with seed pods are dried for using in dry flower arrangements.

Transvaal Daisy

Botanical Name	:	*Arctotis stoechadifolia var. grandis*
Family	:	Compositae
Common Name	:	African Daisy/Transvaal Daisy
Raising of Seedling	:	September-October
Transplanting Month	:	October-November
Planting Distance	:	45 cm x 30 cm
Height of Plant	:	Intermediate: 30-45 cm
Flowering Month	:	February-March
Colours	:	Bronze, orange, salmon, white, ivory and pink
Soil	:	Heavy
Sunlight	:	Full
Irrigation	:	Mild
Suitable For	:	Beddings, pots and borders

Arctotis grandis is bushy and can be grown easily without much care. The stem is erect, cylindrical and green. The leaves are short and thick with deeply cut margins. The daisy-like flower is borne on long stalk having steel-grey colour backed petals.

The seeds takes 7-10 days to germinate and then are transferred to the flower beds. The flowers are sun-loving and appear after 90-120 days of sowing. In hilly areas the sowing time is March-April. The flower remains open only during daytime and closes in the evening.

Arctotis grandis is best sown for its mass effect especially in rock gardens.

English Daisy

Botanical Name	:	*Bellis perennis*
Family	:	Compositae
Common Name	:	English Daisy/Daisy
Raising of Seedling	:	September-October
Transplanting Month	:	October-November
Planting Distance	:	15 cm x 15 cm
Height of Plant	:	Dwarf: 20-30 cm
Flowering Month	:	February-March
Colours	:	Pinkish, white and crimson
Soil	:	Medium
Sunlight	:	Partial
Irrigation	:	Normal
Suitable For	:	Beddings, edging, pots, rock gardens and as cut flowers

Underneath large blue-bells tented where the daises are rose-scented,
And the rose herself has got perfume which on earth is not.
Keats – Bards of Passion and of Mirth

Bellis perennis has a short and thick stem. The leaves are shiny and strap-shaped through which protrude small 3-5 cm single or double flowers.

It is a slow creeping perennial and is grown as annuals in the plains and biennials in the hills where it is sown in February-March. It is a fully hardy plant and survives well in cold temperatures. Seedlings are preferred to suckers. It takes about 100-120 days for the flowers to bloom. Remove the faded flowers regularly to prevent self-seeding. Buds need to be collected almost every day. The seeds come out after 3-4 days of drying in shade.

Bellis perennis decorate low bowls in floral design but they are seldom acknowledged as dried flowers. It is a true English Daisy.

The annual variety is used as mass plantationfor poorly managed gardens and double flower variety is used as loose cut flowers.

Kale

Botanical Name	:	*Brassica oleracea*
Family	:	Cruciferae
Common Name	:	Kale/Decorative Cabbage
Raising of Seedling	:	September-October
Transplanting Month	:	October-November
Planting Distance	:	45 cm x 45 cm
Height of Plant	:	Medium: 30-45 cm
Flowering Month	:	February-March
Colours	:	Purple, violet, green, mixed fringed leaf whorls
Soil	:	Heavy
Sunlight	:	Full
Irrigation	:	Normal
Suitable For	:	Beddings and pots

Flowers seem intended for the solace of ordinary humanity.
John Ruskin

The seeds are sown direct in the flower beds or raised in the nursery. Chilling (cool) temperature bring out most beautiful colours. It makes an attractive pot plant with its colourful foliage for a long period. Prior to its coming into flowering in late April, the flowers are light yellow in colour and remain in bloom for a short period. Foliage is edible and is widely used for salad decoration. It is best used in mass display of colours in rows and undulations.

Swan River Daisy

Botanical Name	:	*Brachycome iberidifolia*
Family	:	Compositae
Common Name	:	Swan River Daisy
Raising of Seedling	:	August-September
Transplanting Month	:	September-November
Planting Distance	:	15 cm x 15 cm
Height of Plant	:	Dwarf: up to 30 cm
Flowering Month	:	February-March
Colours	:	White, azure, blue, purple, pink and yellow
Soil	:	Medium
Sunlight	:	Full
Irrigation	:	Normal
Suitable For	:	Pot flowers, beddings, borders, rockery and edging

When daises pied and violet blue, and lady-smocks all silver-white
and cuckoo-buds of yellow hue do paint the meadows with delight.
Shakespeare – *Love's Labour's Lost*

Brachycome iberidifolia have thin, slender, wiry stem with sprawling habit. The leaves are small and narrow. It is an elegant flower having a string convex centre with a darker disk.

Direct sowing of seeds is preferred to nursery sowing. Pinching should be done to make the plant bushy and to get a thick bloom effect. It takes 90 days for the flowers to appear after transplanting. Plants should be protected from frost during peak winters. They are grown in March-April in the northern hills.

It is best suitable as pot flower because of its profuse, dense flowering.

Calendula

Botanical Name	:	*Calendula officinalis*
Family	:	Compositae
Common Name	:	Calendula/Gulsarfi
Raising of Seedling	:	January-June-September
Transplanting Month	:	February-August-October
Planting Distance	:	30 cm x 30 cm
Height of Plant	:	Medium: 30-45 cm
Flowering Month	:	November-April
Colours	:	Yellow, orange and pastel colours
Soil	:	Heavy
Sunlight	:	Full
Irrigation	:	Normal
Suitable For	:	Bedding, cutting, window-boxes and as pot flowers

Flowers are love's truest language; they betray, like the divining rods of Magi old,
where precious wealth lies buried, not of gold, but love – strong love, that never can decay!
Park Benjamin – 'Sonnet-Flowers', *Love's Truest Language*

The stem of *Calendula officinalis* is erect, herbaceous, branched and coarse. The narrow thin leaves are simple, sessile, alternately arranged and hairy with entire margins. The flowers are borne on long stalks and the florescence is a capitulum. The centre of it may be dark or bearing colour of the ray floret.

It is a very popular plant which is easily cultivated through seeds. Seeds are sown in nursery beds and later transplanted into the flower beds. However, direct sowing can also be done. It takes 90 days to flower and is among the first few to flower in winter.

The flower remains open for 12-15 days. It gives heavy bloom with profuse flowering and is easy to collect seeds and store. The seeds are harvested when the flower has grown to its full size and are then air-dried.

The presence of *Calendula officinalis* brightens up a dull place and is a good cut flower having a vase life of 5-6 days. It is more suitable for low arrangements but in tall arrangements the flower heads borne on weak stems should be supported by thin wire.

China Aster

Botanical Name	:	*Callisterphus chinensis*
Family	:	Compositae
Common Name	:	China Aster
Raising of Seedling	:	September-October
Transplanting Month	:	October-November
Planting Distance	:	30 cm x 30 cm
Height of Plant	:	Medium: 30 cm
Flowering Month	:	February-March
Colours	:	Shades of pink, blue, mauve, purple, dark blue and white
Soil	:	Heavy
Sunlight	:	Full
Irrigation	:	Normal
Suitable For	:	Beddings, window-boxes, pots and as cut flowers

I will be the gladdest thing under the sun!
I will touch a hundred flowers and not pick one.
Edna St. Vincent Millay – *Afternoon on a Hill*

The plant of *Callisterphus chinensis* is dwarf in size and bears flat, ovate and finely cut, edged leaves on irregular margins. Flowers of various sizes and forms spur on all the stems. The florets are grouped together to form a capitulum which appear to be like a number of petals surrounding a yellow centre.

It is a daisy variety which grows well in soil with lime. The plant bears various types of flowers which are classified according to their form. Early and wilt- resistant varieties are advisable to grow. It requires mild irrigation and a well-drained soil. As the plant grows, pinching should be done to make the plant bushy. A fortnightly light application of liquid manure once the bud appears and continuous removal of faded flower gives better and longer bloom. Blooming commences within 14-16 weeks.

The quality of flowers deteriorates as the day temperature sores in April, in the plains. In the hills the sowing period stretches from March-April to August-September.

It is used in floral decorations. The flower is cut along with its stem when the flower begins to appear in its original colour. The flower is used after removing the leaves in the flower arrangement. As an excellent cut flower it lasts for 6-7 days with extraordinary keeping properties. Regular change of water and slicing of the lower part of stem prolongs the cut life to more than a week. The star-shaped calyx (the inner part of the flower) is an attractive dried flower.

It is cultivated for its excellent mass effect and lucrative commercial value.

Corn Flower

Botanical Name	:	*Centaurea cyanus*
Family	:	Compositae
Common Name	:	Corn Flower
Raising of Seedling	:	September-October
Transplanting Month	:	October-November
Planting Distance	:	30 cm x 30 cm
Height of Plant	:	Tall: 60-90 cm
Flowering Month	:	February-March
Colours	:	Blue, pink, white and purple
Soil	:	Medium
Sunlight	:	Full
Irrigation	:	Normal
Suitable For	:	Background, bedding and mixed border

Flowers ... are a proud assertion that a ray of beauty
outvalues all the utilities of the world.
Ralph Waldo Emerson

Centaurea cyanus has a long, erect stem with narrow, grey-green pointed leaves. All the florets are densely grouped together to form a capitulum.

The seeds are sown directly or in nursery beds and take 6-8 days to germinate. The plant starts flowering profusely after 90-100 days and the flowers remain open for 3-4 weeks. Routine garden care is adequate for the upkeep of the plants. The flowering duration can be extended by regular removing of faded flowers. The beauty of blue colour can be exploited by growing them with flowers white or yellow in colour (Calendula). Once the petals fall, collect the seed head which are then air-dried. In the northern hills, they are cultivated in March-April and also in August-October.

The flower suits well as cut flower with vase life of 3-4 days.

Sweet Sultan

Botanical Name	:	*Centaurea moschata*
Family	:	Compositae
Common Name	:	Sweet Sultan
Raising of Seedling	:	September-October
Transplanting Month	:	October-November
Planting Distance	:	30 cm x 30 cm
Height of Plant	:	Tall: 90-100 cm
Flowering Month	:	January-March
Colours	:	Mauve, white and yellow
Soil	:	Medium
Sunlight	:	Full
Irrigation	:	Normal
Suitable For	:	Beddings, herbaceous borders and as cut flowers

Perfumes are the feelings of flowers.
Heinrich Heine – *The Hartz Journey*

The stem of *Centaurea moschata* is long and erect. The leaves are toothed with tapering tips. The flowers (the group of florets) are soft and fluffy and are borne at the tip of thin, wiry and long stems. The flower head is usually very attractive and puff-like possessing heavy fragrance.

Seeds are sown in the nursery beds or direct in the flower beds. The plant is tall, less branching in habit and has a tendency to lean, but it does not require staking. It takes about 90-100 days to bloom. The plant does form an impressive mass effect but also gives a good effect when grown along with other plants in the flower beds. In the hills, it is grown in March-April and August-October.

Sweet Sultan is a highly scented cut flower. It is grown because of its ostentatious appearance and delicate composition.

Wall Flower

Botanical Name	:	*Cheiranthus cheiri*
Family	:	Cruciferae
Common Name	:	Wall Flower
Raising of Seedling	:	September-October
Transplanting Month	:	October-November
Planting Distance	:	30 cm x 15 cm
Height of Plant	:	Medium: 30-45 cm
Flowering Month	:	February-March
Colours	:	Yellow, cream, orange, rust, golden, scarlet, bronze and purple
Soil	:	Light to heavy
Sunlight	:	Full
Irrigation	:	Normal
Suitable For	:	Beddings and as cut flowers

The picture of a flower in a botanical book is information;
its mission ends with our knowledge.
Rabindranath Tagore

Cheiranthus cheiri is medium in size, having thin and erect branches. The leaves are thin, long, alternate, sessile (without petiole) or sub-sessile, the entire margin with tapering tips. A cluster of four-petalled flower appears on the top of the branch. The flowers are arranged in corymbs with cruciform type of corolla, i.e., the four petals are diagonally placed.

It is seldom found in gardens and is commonly seen growing on the walls of old structures in Europe. Hence the name 'Wall Flower'. Only direct sowing is preferred as the plant does not support transplanting. The plant relishes cool long climate; however, protection is required from frost during the peak winter season. Pinching brings another crop of fresh flowers. Blooming of flowers commences within 90-100 days of sowing. The biennials thrive best in hilly areas or in places where there are long winters, i.e., they are sown from February-March and August-October. The flowers are highly fragrant.

Guldaudi

Botanical Name	:	*Chrysanthemum morifolium*
Family	:	Compositae
Common Name	:	Guldaudi
Raising through roots	:	June-August
Transplanting Month	:	July-September
Planting Distance	:	30 cm x 30 cm
Height of Plant	:	Tall: 60-90 cm
Flowering Month	:	November-December
Colours	:	Varied
Soil	:	Light to Heavy
Sunlight	:	Full
Irrigation	:	Heavy
Suitable For	:	Borders, partitions, beds, as cut and pot flowers and for making garlands

The flower is the poetry of reproduction.
It is an example of the eternal seductiveness of life.
Jean Giraudoux

Propagation is done using 'root suckers' and 'terminal cutting'. In the former method, cut the old growth by the end of December and place the plants under shade once the flowering is complete. The root suckers appear in February-March which are separated as they grow 8-10 cm in length and transferred to pots or beds. In April the suckers branch profusely and should be pinched 10-12 cm above the ground to encourage branching. Later in June, the cut portion of suckers are also used for cuttings.

Terminal cuttings yield quality flowers. In February, identify a healthy plant and cut the upper portion. In June, prepare 'terminal cuttings' from the new growth about 4-6 cm in size bearing 3-4 leaves and insert them in the sterilized sand at a distance of 3-4 cm after treating them with growth hormone. Keep them moist and under shade. After 14-21 days, roots start appearing on terminal cuttings and the plant starts showing vigorous growth as the weather becomes warmer in March. Thereafter, pinching is done regularly unto May for the formation of new branches.

During this period, protect the 'terminal cuttings' from the heat of summer by covering under partial shade and keeping them moist. In July (in the plains), once the cuttings are established transfer them into polythene bags of 8-12 cm filled with equal parts of soil and farmyard manure (FYM). Now a days 'plug trays' are also available for the purpose. After 21-28 days, transplant only those cuttings in the soil beds or pots that have shown growth in the polythene bags. This activity is completed by late July to early August.

The plant is also prone to diseases and attacks by insects and pests. So, in the month of September aphids and bugs are killed by Roger 30 EC (dimethoate) @ 2 ml/litre. Leaf spot is more common among all diseases and Dithane M-45 20.2% (fungicide) spray is recommended fortnightly. Leaves infested by hairy caterpillar are destroyed manually when larva is living in groups. American bollworm larva feeds on petals and is killed using Nuvacron 100 (dichlovors) @ 1-2ml/litre in water. Bavistin is effective for fungus and monochorophus for insects. White flies attack during the vegetative growth. The plants need regular application of fertilizers. Liquid fertilizers like 'manusol' can also be used.

In rainy season, remove excessive water from the beds and tilt the pots filled with rainwater. The terminal shoot of well grown plants is pinched, while side buds of standard variety are disbudded. Disbudding, pinching and staking operations vary with variety. In 'standard type', 1-4 large flowers are formed, which are caused by disbudding and pinching and require single staking. A cluster of small flowers is formed in 'spray type' by regular pinching in August-September and needs all round staking.

There is vigorous growth in the month of October, therefore regular irrigation and a fortnightly dose of fertilizer is required. The vegetative phase needs long day treatment while flowering requires short day or long dark hours. Temperature between 15-25 degree Celsius and less than 13½ hours of daylight can bring about heavy growth of flowers. November-December is the period of full bloom. Continuously remove the spent flowers and earmark the best plants for mother stock.

Always select a flower with tight and curled petals. The best quality is available before frost. The cut life of a flower is 8-10 days and all varieties can be used in different styles. In large varieties defoliation is done, as the leaves do not have much relevance to the size of the flower. It is not used as a dry flower.

It is cultivated commercially for its varied colours, shapes and keeping quality. *Chrysanthemum* are grouped as large flowers referred as standard and small flowers referred as sprays. It offers excellent value as a pot flower and gives spectacular mass effect. This type is used as cut flowers (standard varieties), loose flowers, and for making garlands and stylish arrangements (spray varieties). Flower characteristics and growth factor determine the suitability as cut or a pot flower. A short-stemmed flower is best suitable for pots while the longer ones are used in flower arrangements.

Guldaudi

Botanical Name	:	*Chrysanthemum morifolium* (annual)
Family	:	Compositae
Common Name	:	Guldaudi/Jafferi
Raising of Seedling	:	September-October
Transplanting Month	:	October-November
Planting Distance	:	30 cm x 30 cm
Height of Plant	:	Tall: 60-90 cm
Flowering Month	:	February-April
Colours	:	Varied
Soil	:	Light to Heavy
Sunlight	:	Full
Irrigation	:	Heavy
Suitable For	:	Borders, partitions, beds, as cut flowers and for making garlands

Flowers are the beautiful hieroglyphics of nature,
with which she indicates how much she loves us.
Johann Wolfgang von Goethe

The flower bed is raised from cuttings. The annuals and local variety are propagated by sowing seeds and cuttings. Multiplication of Guldaudi is discussed in the previous page.

Clarkia

Botanical Name	:	*Clarikia elegans*
Family	:	Onagraceae
Common Name	:	Clarkia
Raising of Seedling	:	September-October
Transplanting Month	:	September-November
Planting Distance	:	30 cm x 30 cm
Height of Plant	:	Tall: 60-90 cm
Flowering Month	:	February-March
Colours	:	Rose, purple, salmon, scarlet, white and pink
Soil	:	Heavy/Medium
Sunlight	:	Full/Partial
Irrigation	:	Mild
Suitable For	:	Fencing, borders and beddings

A flowerless room is a soulless room, to my way of thinking;
but even one solitary little vase of a living flower may redeem it.
Vita Sackville – West

Clarikia elegans is a tall growing hardy annual with thin, oval-shaped leaves found sparsely on stems. The stem is not very hard, making the plant look lean. The small flowers are single or double and borne on the axils of leaves.

Direct sowing is preferred to seedling. The seeds germinate within 12-14 days. A light irrigation at short intervals is beneficial to over-watering as the plant prefers dry conditions. Pinching should be done to develop side branches and increase the bloom. Staking makes the plant stand erect. The plant flowers within 60-70 days. March-April and August-October are the time to sow the annual in the northern hills.

The flower gains popularity due to its peculiar shape and mass effect.

Coreopsis

Botanical Name	:	*Coreopsis elegans*
Family	:	Compositae
Common Name	:	Coreopsis/Tick Seed
Raising of Seedling	:	September-October
Transplanting Month	:	October-November
Planting Distance	:	30 cm x 30 cm
Height of Plant	:	Tall: 60-90 cm
Flowering Month	:	January-April
Colours	:	Yellow with maroon centre and pure yellow
Soil	:	Medium
Sunlight	:	Full
Irrigation	:	Normal
Suitable For	:	Beddings, borders and as cut flowers

To see a world in a Grain of Sand, And a Heaven in a Wild Flower,
Hold Infinity in the palm of your hand, And eternity in an hour.
William Blake

The flower of *Coreopsis elegans* looks attractive with a contrast of dark brown in the centre and yellow colour towards the border. It is a hardy annual with long hollow stem which has tendency to lean and thus requires staking. The entire flower bed can be supported by using a cord tied on either side of the flower bed. There arise as many as 16-22 main branches from the main stem which further produce 4-6 flower-bearing secondary stems.

Coreopsis does not require much care and is easy to grow. Direct sowing is preferred. It is cultivated throughout the year but does not yield bloom during extreme cold climate. The flowers appear within 50-60 days. The winter crop when pruned up to 12-18 inches from ground level towards their end life can yield another bloom till June. However, the bloom lasts for a short duration. Once the bloom is over and the flower head turns brown, withhold watering for 4-5 days prior to seed collection. Cut the stem 15-20 cm above the ground and collect the seeds thereafter.

Coreopsis is well identified as a cut flower having a cut life of 4-6 days. The long, thin and weak stem needs wire support when used in Western style of floral arrangements. Coreopsis has an impressive mass effect.

Cosmos

Botanical Name	:	*Cosmos bipinnatus*
Family	:	Compositae
Common Name	:	Cosmos/Mexican Aster
Raising of Seedling	:	September-October
Transplanting Month	:	October-November
Planting Distance	:	45 cm x 45 cm
Height of Plant	:	Tall: 60-90 cm
Flowering Month	:	January-March
Colours	:	Magenta, mauve, white, pink, crimson
Soil	:	Medium
Sunlight	:	Full
Irrigation	:	Normal
Suitable For	:	Beddings, borders and as cut flowers

Every flower is a soul blossoming in nature.
Gerard De Nerval

Cosmos bipinnatus is a tall plant having well-branched wiry stems. The leaves are long, thin, feathery and deeply cut. The central petals form a tuft-like cluster of the flower head while broad and long ray florets remain in the background.

Cosmos is a hardy and robust plant which can be grown throughout the year in adverse, warm and humid conditions. The seeds are sown in the nursery beds and later transplanted to the flower beds but direct sowing is recommended. The seeds take 6-14 days to germinate. Heavy dose of manure causes growth of foliage and curtails the growth of flowers. Flowers start appearing within 50-60 days. *C. sulphureus* is economical to grow and easy to maintain in comparison to *C. bipinnatus*.

The flower has a cut life of 4-5 days and can be used in tall arrangements.

Cosmos is a popular annual as it is easy to propagate and gives a good mass effect.

Dahlia

Botanical Name	:	*Dahlia variabilis* (from cutting)
Family	:	Compositae
Common Name	:	Dahlia
Raising of Seedling	:	August-November
Transplanting Month	:	September-October
Planting Distance	:	45 cm x 45 cm
Height of Plant	:	Medium to tall
Flowering Month	:	January-April
Colours	:	White, red, yellow, mauve, crimson and varied shades
Soil	:	Medium to heavy
Sunlight	:	Full
Irrigation	:	Heavy
Suitable For	:	Beddings, borders and pots

Dahlia variabilis is a tuberous rooted perennial and is classified into almost a dozen types. Plants with heavy bloom and big size need more care, extra manure, frequent watering and proper staking. Pots need frequent watering while those on the ground may require heavy watering at long intervals, depending upon the climate and type of soil. Protection from frost is required.

To keep the plant bushy, pinching should be done at the tip of the healthy plants. Once the plant is nearing its full size, multiple staking in triangle or square form is done around the pot on the main and side branches of the plant. When grown in beds, two or three rows of supporting wires are used. Use soft material and apply loose knots so as to enable the plant to gain width. Retain the main bud and disbud the other as soon as they appear to get a good bloom. If required, side shoots can also be removed.

Limited propagation is done by uprooting mature tubers. Store the tubers after cleaning with Bavistan in a cool and moist place under shade, in the mud or indoors. 'Division of tuber' is done in a way that each tuber contains the portion of stem with a vegetative bud. The tubers are then planted directly in the field 12-15 cm deep and 45 cm x 60 cm apart in August. The flowers appear in November/December.

In September-November, the 'terminal cuttings' are prepared from the young, healthy shoots which are detached close to the crown below the node. After removing the lower leaves, treat it with Seradix-1 and plant in mixture of sand and leaf mould. Roots generally appear within 2-3 weeks of sowing and thereafter shifted in the beds or pots.

Dahlia is very popular as a pot plant in flower shows.

Dahlia

*Flower in the crannied wall, I pluck you out of the crannies,
I hold you here, root and all, in my hand, Little flower-but if I could understand
What you are, root and all, and all in all, I should know what God and man is.*
Tennyson

Botanical Name	:	*Dahlia variabilis* (through seeds)
Family	:	Compositae
Common Name	:	Dahlia
Raising of Seedling	:	August-September
Transplanting Month	:	September-October
Planting Distance	:	45 cm x 45 cm
Height of Plant	:	Dwarf-Tall: 90-120 cm
Blooming Month	:	January-February
Flower Duration	:	21-28 days
Colours	:	White, red, yellow, mauve, crimson and varied shades
Soil	:	Heavy
Sunlight	:	Full
Irrigation	:	Heavy
Suitable For	:	Beddings, borders and pots

For propagation details, see previous page.

Larkspur

Botanical Name	:	*Delphinium ajacis*
Family	:	Ranunculaceae
Common Name	:	Larkspur
Raising of Seedling	:	September-October
Transplanting Month	:	October-November
Planting Distance	:	30 cm x 30 cm
Height of Plant	:	Tall: 60-90 cm
Flowering Month	:	February-March
Colours	:	Pink, blue, white, violet and shades of red
Soil	:	Heavy
Sunlight	:	Full
Irrigation	:	Normal
Suitable For	:	Screening, hedges, along the wall, borders, background and dwarf varieties in pots. It is an excellent cut flower.

Blue thou art, intensely blue;
Flower, whence came thy dazzling hue?
Montogomery – *The Gentianella*

Delphinium ajacis is a tall, erect plant, thin with sturdy stem having many branches bearing flower spikes. The leaves have deeply cut lobes.

The plant is hardy which can be grown as annuals in the northern plains. Direct sowing of seeds in the flower bed or propagation in 'plug tray' is preferred. The seeds are sown in nursery beds and later transplanted to flower beds. When the flowers begin to wither, cut the top-most part of the stem above 60 cm from the ground. It can yield a second bloom till the time the weather remains cool. The stemmed spike with a cluster of spurred flowers may get damaged if detached carelessly.

The tall flowers of Larkspur form excellent fillers in large arrangements and as line arrangements in Western type of flower arrangements. The spike has a cut life of 6-7 days. The seed head is picked and air-drying is done following the fall of petals.

It is used as a cut flower. Larkspur is a good screening material and its blue colour adds variety to the garden.

Sweet William

Botanical Name	:	*Dianthus barbatus*
Family	:	Caryophyllaceae
Common Name	:	Sweet William
Raising of Seedling	:	September-October
Transplanting Month	:	October-November
Planting Distance	:	30 cm x 30 cm
Height of Plant	:	Medium: 30-45 cm
Flowering Month	:	February-March
Colours	:	Mauve, crimson, pink, scarlet, purple and white
Soil	:	Heavy/Medium
Sunlight	:	Full
Irrigation	:	Normal
Suitable For	:	Beddings, borders, rockery, pots and as cut flowers

To me the meanest flower that blows can give
Thoughts that do often lie too deep for tears.
Wordsworth – *Intimations of Immortality*

The stem of *Dianthus barbatus* is firm and erect spreading at the top. The leaves are elongated and flat with pointed tips. The edged flowers grow on top of the branches forming an eye-catching flowering head.

The species is biennial but is commonly grown as annuals in North India. It requires a rich and well-drained soil. Direct sowing of seed can also be done against the standard practice of raising seedlings. The annual strain bears single or double flowers in clusters at the apex of the branches. Flowering takes place after 90-100 days. The dead flowers should be regularly removed to prolong the blooming period.

Sweet William has good value as a cut flower filler due to dense flowering at the apex. The flower does not go well with other flowers because of its multi-coloured medium-sized flowers. It is best suited for low vase and for mass floral arrangements. The flowers are air-dried when utilized as dried flowers. Sweet William is known to have a very pleasant fragrance.

Carnation

Botanical Name	:	*Dianthus caryphyllus*
Family	:	Caryophyllaceae
Common Name	:	Carnation
Raising of Seedling	:	October-November
Transplanting Month	:	November-December
Planting Distance	:	30 cm x 30 cm
Height of Plant	:	Medium: 45-60 cm
Flowering Month	:	February-March
Colours	:	Yellow, white, pink, red and bio-colours
Soil	:	Heavy
Sunlight	:	Full
Irrigation	:	Normal
Suitable For	:	Beddings, pots and as cut flowers

Gardens are not made by sitting in the shade.
Rudyard Kipling

Dianthus caryphyllus is a medium-sized plant with thin and sleek, greyish-green stem having two small lanceolate leaves at each node. The flower buds are borne terminally in three. Usually two buds are removed to allow the central growing bud to get better bloom.

Carnation is very common and much valued in Europe. It is considered as an annual in the plains and perennial in the northern hills. The plant appears like a shrub and is propagated both through seeds (in October-November) and cuttings taken from the side shoots. Single varieties are propagated by seeds which germinate within 7-8 days and double varieties are propagated by cutting. The cuttings are sown as terminal cutting in September and transplanted in mid-October. As the stem is weak, continuous staking is required while sowing in a pot ensures that the coverage is uniform and the

growth is compact. The seedlings need protection during extreme climatic conditions in peak summers, heavy rains, high-speed winds and winters. Pinching encourages growth of side branches and hardening of the stem while disbudding at an early stage causes the flowers to grow in size. A dose of fertilizer after pinching and when buds appear yields good results. The bloom commences after 100-120 days.

It is used extensively because of the beautiful flower and long cut life of 6-7 days. Cut the flower above or below the joints on the stems and give a deep drink. The beautiful flowers in medium size stems look impressive in various styles of floral arrangements.

Carnation is mildly clove scented, attractive and is most admired for its colour and form with good commercial value.

Pink

Botanical Name	:	*Dianthus chinensis*
Family	:	Caryophyllaceae
Common Name	:	Pink
Raising of Seedling	:	September-October
Transplanting Month	:	October-November
Planting Distance	:	30 cm x 15 cm
Height of Plant	:	Medium: 30-60 cm
Flowering Month	:	December-March
Colours	:	White, pink, red, maroon, crimson and mixed colours
Soil	:	Heavy
Sunlight	:	Full
Irrigation	:	Normal
Suitable For	:	Beddings, borders, edging, pots and as cut flowers

*When you take a flower in your hand and really look at it, it's your world for the moment
I want to give that world to someone else. Most people in the city rush around so,
they have no time to look at a flower. I want them to see it whether they want to or not.*
Georgia O'keeffe

Dainthus chinensis is fully hardy, evergreen plant the composition of which is quite close to Phlox. Small double flowers grow in clusters on medium size stems. The leaves are small and smooth with tapering tips. The flowers appear in clusters at the end of the edges on the tip of the stem forming large heads.

Pink and Carnation are preferred by many gardeners and have similarity in appearance and habit. They are long day plants for vegetative growth and flowering. Pinching at very early stage makes the plant well-branched and bushy. Flowering takes place after 100-120 days of transplanting.

The flowers are scented and are most suited for pots due to their dense top coverage effect.

African Daisy

Botanical Name	:	*Dimorphotheca aurantiaca*
Family	:	Compositae
Common Name	:	African Daisy
Raising of Seedling	:	September-October
Transplanting Month	:	October-November
Planting Distance	:	30 cm x 30 cm
Height of Plant	:	Medium: 30-45 cm
Flowering Month	:	February-March
Colours	:	Dazzling white, shades of yellow, orange and purple
Soil	:	Heavy/Medium
Sunlight	:	Full
Irrigation	:	Normal
Suitable For	:	Beddings and pots

Full many a flowers is born to blush unseen,
And waste their sweetness on the desert air.
Gray – *Elegy Written in a Country Churchyard*

Dimorphotheca aurantiaca is compact, bushy in composition with thin, narrow leaves and toothed or entire margin. The flowers appear on the terminals of the stems. The dark brown disc in the centre of the flower surrounded by vibrant colours makes the flower look more attractive. However, in some varieties the colour of the disc is variable.

It is a beautiful flower which opens in sunlight and closes at night or on cloudy days. It takes 50-60 days for the flowers to appear. The plant needs protection from frost and cold during the early growth period.

African Daisy is good for rockery, pot plant and is grown for a striking mass effect.

California Poppy

Botanical Name	:	*Eschscholzia californica*
Family	:	Papaveraceae
Common Name	:	California Poppy
Raising of Seedling	:	September-October
Transplanting Month	:	Not Transplanted
Planting Distance	:	30 cm x 30 cm
Height of Plant	:	Medium: 45 cm
Flowering Month	:	January-March
Colours	:	Orange, yellow, red, crimson, white, cream and lemon
Soil	:	Light and sandy
Sunlight	:	Full
Irrigation	:	Normal
Suitable For	:	Beddings, pots, along pavements and as cut flowers for short durations

In Flanders field the poppies blow, between the crosses row on row,
That mark our place; and in the sky, the larks, still bravely singing,
fly scare heard among the guns below.
John McCrae – *In the Flanders' Field*

Eschscholzia californica has a semi-erect, slender and long stem, having finely-cut smooth grey-green leaves. Flowers are single coloured or bi-coloured with peculiar open cup or saucer shape which are single, semi-double or double.

It is a common annual which is actually a perennial. The plant is easy to grow and requires little care. Seeds are sown directly in the flower beds and later thinning is done. The flower takes 120 days to bloom but gives a short blooming with continuous profusion. The flower closes at night and sheds its petals once faded. After the bloom seeds are collected at regular intervals and later segregation is done accordingly.

Blanket Flower

Botanical Name	:	*Gaillardia pulchella*
Family	:	Compositae
Common Name	:	Blanket Flower
Raising of Seedling	:	September-October
Transplanting Month	:	November
Planting Distance	:	45 cm x 30 cm
Height of Plant	:	Medium: 30-45 cm
Flowering Month	:	February-April
Colours	:	Yellow, orange, brown, cream and scarlet
Soil	:	Medium
Sunlight	:	Full
Irrigation	:	Normal
Suitable For	:	Beddings, borders and as cut flowers

Pluck not the wayside flower; It is the traveler's dower.
William Allingham

The stem of this plant is thin and bears smooth, long leaves. The flowers consist of serrated petals encircling the dark colour centre.

Gaillardia pulchella is perennial in hills and the hardiest annual on northern plains that can be grown on any soil and sown throughout the year in summer (February-March), rainy season (May-June) and in winters (September-October). The seeds take about 14-21 days to germinate.

Blooming takes place after 90-120 days which can be prolonged by regularly withdrawing faded flowers. The flower head is ready for seed collection when the colour changes to greyish straw colour. Thereafter, the flower heads are collected just before the dispersal of the seeds.

Gaillardia pulchella is widely grown as it is easy to propagate and forms heavy mass effect and thick foliage.

Matricaria

Botanical Name	:	*Gamolepsis tagetets*
Family	:	Compositae
Common Name	:	Matricaria/Gamolepsis
Raising of Seedling	:	September
Transplanting Month	:	September-November
Planting Distance	:	30 cm x 30 cm
Height of Plant	:	Dwarf: 30 cm
Flowering Month	:	January-March
Colours	:	Yellow
Soil	:	Medium
Sunlight	:	Full
Irrigation	:	Normal
Suitable For	:	Beddings and as pot flowers

There is that in the glance of a flower,
which may at times control the greatest of creation's braggart lords.
John Muir – A Thousand-Mile Walk to the Gulf, 1916

Gamolepsis tagetets is a half-hardy plant, dwarf in size. The thin wiry leaves are fine and deeply cut. Ray florets are distinct and uniformly shaped around the disc floret. The petals of ray floret are notched at the tip.

The seedlings are produced in nursery beds but seeds can also be sown directly in the flower beds followed by thinning of the dense plantation. The plant is spreading in habit and the flora completely dominates the foliage and gives a yellow carpet effect. It is best sown as a pot plant and for its mass effect.

Treasure Flower

Botanical Name	:	*Gazania splendens*
Family	:	Compositae
Common Name	:	Treasure Flower
Raising of Seedling	:	September-October
Transplanting Month	:	October-November
Planting Distance	:	30 cm x 30 cm
Height of Plant	:	Dwarf: 30 cm
Flowering Month	:	January-March
Colours	:	Pink, orange, yellow, white, brown and mixed shades
Soil	:	Medium
Sunlight	:	Full
Irrigation	:	Normal
Suitable For	:	Beddings, edging, rockeries and as pot flowers

I am following Nature without being able to grasp her.
I perhaps owe having become a painter to flowers.
Claude Monet

Gazania splendens is trailing in habit and bears silvery long, narrow leaves with pointed end. The leaves have wooly hair on the underside. The flowers have a large surface area and are exceedingly showy with spectacular looks. The ray petals of the flowers have contrasting colours.

Multiplication of plant is done by sowing of seeds direct in the flower beds. The flower takes 90-100 days to bloom but thereafter continues flowering for a long period. The flower is unique as it closes in late afternoon or in dull weather as the intensity of the sunshine reduces. Winter rainfall is not good for the plant. De-head the flower regularly to encourage flowering. Fruits (cypsela) are collected regularly and seeds are collected after 3-4 days of drying.

It is especially suitable for growing in rock gardens. The flower is extremely elegant bearing sharp colour strips.

Gerbera

Botanical Name	:	*Gerbera jamesonii*
Family	:	Compositae
Common Name	:	Gerbera
Raising of Seedling	:	September-October/February-March
Transplanting Month	:	October-November
Planting Distance	:	40 cm x 30 cm
Height of Plant	:	Medium: 30-45 cm
Flowering Month	:	Almost round the year
Colours	:	Pink, red, orange, yellow, white, lilac
Soil	:	Medium
Sunlight	:	Partial shade
Irrigation	:	Normal
Suitable For	:	Raised beds and as cut flowers

Flowers always make people better, happier and more helpful; they are sunshine, food and medicine to the soul.
Luther Burbank

Gerbera jamesonii has a small stem with broad leaves which are narrow towards the base and broad at the tip with deeply cut edges. The flower head consists of long ray and disc florets. The petals are long, narrow, compactly arranged and surround the inner dark circle. The flower can be single or double.

The plant is a herbaceous perennial which grows in clumps. The roots of Gerbera go very deep in the soil, therefore raised soil beds about 12-15 cm are prepared by deep digging up to 30 cm. In September, the large clumps are divided into small clumps and planted. In February, the clump from the mother plant gives rise to 5-6 plants. Keeping the main shoot intact, trim the roots and leaves of the suckers and bury the main shoot in such a way that the main shoot does not get covered by the soil. The hot summer is harmful to Gerbera so it needs to be protected from direct sunlight using nets or the plant can be grown under the partial shade of trees in the vicinity.

Freshly harvested seeds in March-April should be sown in beds and planted in 4 inch size pots till they reach 1-2 inch in size. The pots are maintained under shade till their final transplanting in beds during September-October. Transplantation is done when the seedlings attain a height of 4-5 inch.

It is a popular, attractive and ideal cut flower having a cut life of 6-8 days.

Satin Flower

Botanical Name	:	*Godetia grandiflora*
Family	:	Onagraceae
Common Name	:	Satin Flower/Farewell-to-Spring
Raising of Seedling	:	August-September
Transplanting Month	:	September-November
Planting Distance	:	30 cm x 45 cm
Height of Plant	:	Medium: 30-45 cm
Flowering Month	:	September-November
Colours	:	Rose, deep pink and white, with a blotch in the centre
Soil	:	Medium
Sunlight	:	Full
Irrigation	:	Medium
Suitable For	:	Pots and borders

To be overcome by the fragrance of flowers is a delectable form of defeat.
Beverly Nichols

Godetia grandiflora is a hardy annual with bushy growth. It is suitable for medium-high elevations. Prefer direct sowing to raising of nursery. The plant prefers long day conditions. The flowers profuse in masses. The plant makes its presence felt when sown against green herbaceous borders.

To cash the beauty of the shades in the flowers, the cut flower must be placed in contrast with other flowers. The mass effect of Satin flower is eye-catching.

Baby's Breath

Botanical Name	:	*Gypsophila elegans*
Family	:	Caryophyllaceae
Common Name	:	Baby's Breath/Chalk Plant
Raising of Seedling	:	September-October
Transplanting Month	:	October-November
Planting Distance	:	30 cm x 20 cm
Height of Plant	:	Medium: 45-60 cm
Flowering Month	:	February-April
Colours	:	White, pink and purple
Soil	:	Light to medium
Sunlight	:	Full
Irrigation	:	Normal
Suitable For	:	Beddings and as cut flowers

Little things seem nothing, but they give peace,
like those meadow
which individually seem odorless but all together perfume the air.
Georges Bernanos

It is a low-growing annual having long, thin and multi-branched stem bearing tiny leaves. The flower hangs in clusters towards the tip of the stem. The flowers are single or double, tiny, showy and delicate.

The plant is easy to grow and needs little care. A cool climate is always preferred to hot. Blooming after 90-110 days gives a mass effect comprising a cluster of white flowers which covers the entire flower bed. To enjoy continuous flowering sow them at regular intervals.

Gypsophila elegans is not common in home gardens but forms eye-catching, dense, lacy filler in bouquet or floral designs. The flowers sparkle in the vicinity when used with contrasting colours. The plant does not flourish well in low elevations. It serves as a good appetizer for rabbits.

Gypsophila elegans has a cut life of seven days and should be detached from the parent plant when the flower is fully open but not over-matured.

It is appreciated for its sparkling appearance, mist-like spray and usage as an outstanding filler.

Everlasting Flower

Botanical Name	:	*Helichrysum bracteatum*
Family	:	Compositae
Common Name	:	Everlasting Flower/Straw Flower
Raising of Seedling	:	September-October
Transplanting Month	:	October-November
Planting Distance	:	30 cm x 30 cm
Height of Plant	:	Tall: 60-90 cm
Flowering Month	:	February-March
Colours	:	White, pink, yellow, peach and crimson
Soil	:	Medium
Sunlight	:	Full
Irrigation	:	Normal
Suitable For	:	Beddings, borders, as cut flowers and especially as dry flowers

Keep a green tree in your heart and perhaps the singing bird will come.
Chinese Proverb

The stem is stiff, erect and herbaceous. The small florets are incurved and arranged in the flower heads. The petals are compactly arranged with tapering tips. The flowers are papery in texture and the flower heads are dry hence known as Paper Flower/Straw Flower.

The plant needs little care and has wide adaptability. It is a widely grown, free-flowering, tall annual. The seeds are sown in nursery beds and later transplanted into the flower beds. Over-manuring contributes only to the vegetative growth and not to the size of the flower. The flowers appear within 100-110 days of sowing and remain open for 21-30 days. At the seed collection stage the receptacle bearing seeds turn greyish-brown in colour and begin to fall at the slightest touch.

As a mature flower it retains both colour and form and lasts for a very long period and, therefore, it is commonly known as 'everlasting flower'. The flower is picked up when half mature when is to be used as cut flower. It is also used as a dry flower after defoliating the leaves. The monotony of the floral design and settling of dust on the flower makes its presence unattractive and lowers the viewer interest after a specific time period.

Candytuft

Botanical Name	:	*Iberis amara*
Family	:	Cruciferae
Common Name	:	Candytuft/Hyacinth Flower
Raising of Seedling	:	September-October
Transplanting Month	:	October-November
Planting Distance	:	30 cm x 20 cm
Height of Plant	:	Medium: 30-45 cm
Flowering Month	:	February-March
Colours	:	White, pink and purple
Soil	:	Medium
Sunlight	:	Full
Irrigation	:	Normal
Suitable For	:	Edging, beddings, borders, hanging, pots and as cut flowers

The temple bell stops
but I still hear the sound coming out of the flowers.
Basho

The stem of *Iberis amara* is erect, herbaceous and branching in habit. The leaves are small, long, and narrow with a smooth surface. The stocked flower (pedicilate) is arranged in an acropetal manner forming flat clusters borne at the tip of the branches in a flat/cylindrical formation. It is a popular free-flowering annual.

An amateur gardener may find close resemblance among Sweet Alyssum and Candytuft. It is a medium annual and very popularly used along borders and paths. Soil rich in lime best suits the plant. The flowers grow lavishly and completely dominate the foliage after 90-100 days. The snow white colour of the flower gives a cool carpet effect to the eye.

The flower has a cut life of only 4-5 days. The white colour makes an ideal combination with dark colours in floral designs. If not uprooted, the flower dries up naturally and is then used as dry flower.

Candytuft is a good filler and gives a picturesque effect to the garden.

Sweet Pea

Botanical Name	:	*Lathyrus odoratus*
Family	:	Leguminosae
Common Name	:	Sweet Pea
Raising of Seedling	:	September-October
Transplanting Month	:	October-November
Planting Distance	:	Refer to cultivation note*
Height of Plant	:	Tall: 60-90 cm
Flowering Month	:	February-March
Colours	:	White, pink, red, blue, lilac, mauve, salmon or maroon
Soil	:	Medium
Sunlight	:	Full
Irrigation	:	Normal, slightly saline
Suitable For	:	Screening and can be trained on stumps

Bread feeds the body, indeed, but flowers feed also the soul.
The Koran

Lathyrus odoratus has a weak, slightly hairy and a hollow stem. The leaves are thin and long and the upper leaflets are modified into tendrils which coil around the support. A typical papitionaceous corolla encloses the essential parts of the flower. This arrangement leads to self-pollination.

*Soak the seeds overnight in water. Thereafter, sow them directly on the midway of the slope of the prepared raised bed 15-20 cm apart and 2-3 cm deep in a single row. When sown in double rows, keep a distance of 35 cm from one row to another. Fill the channels with water till the water moists the top level. Thereafter, regularly irrigate to keep the soil moist and avoid water logging. A shady location will produce a weak plant and few flowers.

The annual climber bears large, delicate and neat flowers with a pretty look after 80-90 days. Chilling and cool temperature brings out the most beautiful colours. The supporting material can be wire strings tied parallel on wooden or metallic poles, wire nettings or 'sarkanda' sticks. It requires long exposure to sun during the day. A nicely trained sweet pea gives tidy look to the garden and makes an attractive background. There are about six strains of Lathyrus.

The cut life of the flower is 4-6 days and it is used only for preparing table bowls. Sweet Pea is admired for its form, fragrance and colourful screening effect.

Statice

Botanical Name	:	*Limonium sinuatum*
Family	:	Plumbaginaceae
Common Name	:	Statice/Sea-Pink/Sea-Lavender
Raising of Seedling	:	September-October
Transplanting Month	:	October-November
Planting Distance	:	30 cm x 30 cm
Height of Plant	:	Tall: 60-90 cm
Flowering Month	:	March-April
Colours	:	Peach, white, yellow, purple, pink, mauve, lavender and dark blue
Soil	:	Medium
Sunlight	:	Full
Irrigation	:	Mild
Suitable For	:	Beddings, dry arrangements and as cut flowers

Can we conceive what humanity would be
if it did not know the flowers?
Maurice Maeterlinck

The stems of *Limonium sinuatum* are hardy, angular-branched and carry clusters of flowers on stalks which are winged. The leaves are long, deeply cut, leathery and deeply lobed having a grey-green colour. The flowers have a papery texture and are linear in form.

Statice derives its common name from its natural habitat of select species around the sea coast. A biennial grown as annual, it gives excellent bloom after 90-100 days in a well-drained soil. A contrasting background is desirable as the branch does not have luxuriant foliage.

The entire plant retains its form and colour even on drying for a long time therefore it is best used as a dry flower by making everlasting nature of arrangement. The flowers are air-dried before the flower head fully opens by hanging them upside down. The flowers are also considered as good fillers in fresh and dry floral designs.

Linaria

Botanical Name	:	*Linaria maroccana*
Family	:	Scrophulariaceae
Common Name	:	Linaria/Toad Flax
Raising of Seedling	:	September-October
Transplanting Month	:	October-November
Planting Distance	:	30 cm x 40 cm
Height of Plant	:	Medium: 30-45 cm
Flowering Month	:	January-March
Colours	:	Purple, blue, white, light yellow and pink
Soil	:	Medium/Sandy
Sunlight	:	Full/Partial
Irrigation	:	Mild
Suitable For	:	Beddings, borders and rockery/rock garden

Sweet letters of the angel tongue, I've loved ye long and well, And never have failed in your fragrance sweet
To find some secret spell, – A charm that has bound me with witching power, For mine is the old belief,
That midst your sweets and midst your bloom, There's a soul in every leaf!
Mathurin M. Ballou

Linaria maroccana is a hardy plant, small in height and is erect in habit with thin branches. The thin leaves grow on the erect branches. The tiny flowers appear on these branches giving it a typical look. The plant is free-flowering in habit.

Pinching on the side branches makes the plant bushy. Flowering commences 90-100 days after sowing. Excessive irrigation must be avoided.

Linaria maroccana is a beautiful cut flower useful in the decoration of bouquets and vases.

Linum

Botanical Name	:	*Linum grandiflorum*
Family	:	Linacea
Common Name	:	Linum/Scarlet Flax
Raising of Seedling	:	September-October
Transplanting Month	:	Direct sowing preferred
Planting Distance	:	30 cm x 40 cm
Height of Plant	:	Medium: 30-45 cm
Blooming Month	:	January-March
Colours	:	Scarlet
Soil	:	Medium
Sunlight	:	Full
Irrigation	:	Mild
Suitable For	:	Beddings and borders

Your voiceless lip, O, flowers are living preacher –
each cup a pulpit, and each leaf a book.
Horace Smith

Linum grandiflorum is also commonly known as Scarlet Flax/Linum. It has its origin in Europe and parts of North Africa. The plant bears scarlet flowers with a dark centre. The leaves are narrow and pointed towards the tip.

Seeds are sown direct in the flower beds as they yield better results than being transplanted from nursery beds. Thinning of seedling is done after two to three weeks of germination. A dose of liquid manure is beneficial when buds appear. The flower appears after 90-100 days.

In the hills of northern India, the plant is grown from August to October and March to April.

Sweet Alyssum

Botanical Name	:	*Lobularia maritima*
Family	:	Cruciferae
Common Name	:	Sweet Alyssum/Bajri
Raising of Seedling	:	September-October
Transplanting Month	:	October-November
Planting Distance	:	15 cm x 15 cm
Height of Plant	:	Dwarf: 20-30 cm
Flowering Month	:	November-April
Colours	:	Varied colours
Soil	:	Medium/Loamy
Sunlight	:	Full/Partial
Irrigation	:	Normal
Suitable For	:	Edging, borders, beddings, window boxes and as pot flowers

The snowdrops and primrose our woodlands adorn,
And violet bathe in the wet o' the morn.
Burns – *My Nannie's Awa'*

Lobularia maritima is erect, cylindrical, branched, and herbaceous. The leaves are alternate, long, narrow and green in colour. Every branch bears a spike of white flowers arranged in corymbs which collectively form a carpet of flowers.

The plant is low-growing and spreading in nature. Prefer direct sowing to raising of nursery. Avoid over-irrigation as the plant cannot withstand excess watering. It takes 40-45 days for the flowers to bloom after transplantation. The flowers cover the tiny leaves during a full bloom. To prolong the blooming period continuously remove the spent flowers. Cut the stem a few inches above the ground after the first bloom and add manure to facilitate a second bloom. The seedpods are collected at regular intervals when they turn brown in colour and later seeds are collected. April-May and September-October in the mild climate of South India is the period to cultivate Alyssum while in the northern hills it is sown in February-March.

Grow Alyssum to have a garden full of fragrance and butterflies.

Lupin

Botanical Name	:	*Lupinus hartwegii*
Family	:	Leguminosae
Common Name	:	Lupin
Raising of Seedling	:	September-October
Transplanting Month	:	October-November
Planting Distance	:	30 cm x 30 cm
Height of Plant	:	Tall: 60-75 cm
Flowering Month	:	March-April
Colours	:	Peach, white, yellow, purple, pink, mauve, lavender and dark blue
Soil	:	Medium
Sunlight	:	Full/Partial Shade
Irrigation	:	Light
Suitable For	:	Beddings, borders and pots

People from a planet without flowers would think we must be
mad with joy the whole time to have such things about us.
Iris Murdoch – *A Fairly Honourable Defeat*

The stems of *Lupinus hartwegii* are hardy and the leaves are deeply cut clumps having grey-green colour with hairy surface. The plants have palm-shaped foliage. The spikes of the flowers are borne above the foliage on the entire length of the long stalks.

Soak the large oval-shaped seeds overnight before sowing directly in the flower beds or in nursery beds. It is an annual that blooms in 90-110 days. It thrives best in cool climate as short and mild winters do not produce large flower spikes. Pinch off the tops as soon as the lower pods grow to their full size to avoid the pods from shrivelling. The perennial species seeds are sown in the northern hills in March-April. The plant can also be multiplied by division or cutting.

The dried flower retains its colour for a long time while the cut flower is used as a filler in flower arrangements.

Stock

Botanical Name	:	*Matthiola incana*
Family	:	Cruciferae
Common Name	:	Stock/Gilli Flower
Raising of Seedling	:	September-October
Transplanting Month	:	October-November
Planting Distance	:	30 cm x 30 cm
Height of Plant	:	Tall: 45-60 cm
Flowering Month	:	February-March
Colours	:	White, red, pink, lavender, mauve and crimson
Soil	:	Medium
Sunlight	:	Full/Partial
Irrigation	:	Normal
Suitable For	:	Borders, beds, herbaceous borders, pots and as cut flowers

A root is a flower that disdains fame.
Kahlil Gibran

Matthiola incana is a tall plant with erect growth having a long stem, the branches of which emerge from the base of the plant. The leaves are single, long, narrow, hairy and dark green in colour. The flowers are arranged on the long stalk. The plant bears single flowers, which have four petals and pistil having 25-50 ovules. It also sets seeds which are collected for further propagation. The double flower is sterile, having 45-60 petals. The double character is a genetic factor and has been linked to the light-green colour of the cotyledon.

Stock is available in two forms, branching and non-branching. A cool climate with sunlight yields dense flower spikes and high percentage of double florets. Avoid over-irrigation as it spoils the plant. Precaution should be taken to protect it from 'damping off'. The plant takes 100-110 days to flower which is followed by great profusion.

Bruising the cut ends extends the cut life of the flower. Stocks form ideal cut flowers and are placed in tall or low bowls arrangements. The flower is much admired for its fragrance.

Ice-Plant

Botanical Name	:	*Mesembryanthemum criniflorum*
Family	:	Aizoaceae
Common Name	:	Ice-Plant/Baraf
Raising of Seedling	:	September-October
Transplanting Month	:	October-November
Planting Distance	:	15 cm x 20 cm
Height of Plant	:	Dwarf: 10-15 cm
Flowering Month	:	February-March
Colours	:	Pink, white, yellow, purple and peach
Soil	:	Medium
Sunlight	:	Full
Irrigation	:	Normal
Suitable For	:	Sunny areas, edging, rockery, pots and hanging baskets

Look at us, said the violets blooming at her feet, all last winter we slept in the seeming death
but at the right time God awakened us, and here we are to comfort you.
Edward Payson Rod

The plant is a half-hardy annual, low-growing and trailing with compact growth. The branches are succulent while the leaves are fleshy, thick and elongated. The flowers are single with dark brown centre disc surrounded by either single or multi-coloured rings of colours.

Ice-Plant is popularly known as '9 to 5' plant. The seeds are sown in the nursery beds or direct in the flower beds where the seeds take 12-14 days to germinate. When 4-6 leaves appear thinning is done to maintain the required plant-to-plant distance. It survives in poor soil under dry and sunny locations. The flowers are colourful and showy which open fully under the bright sunshine and close in cloudy weather or at night. In cold winter nights, dew formation on the flower shine like crystals in the morning sunlight. All flowers appear together and accordingly mature and perish at the same time. The ripe buds do not open once fully mature; they are hard to crack, thus broken mechanically to release the seeds. To have a striking effect, grow it on a gradient at a most prominent sunny place in the garden.

The flower exhibits a beautiful, sparkling, shining colourful mass effect and provides good ground cover.

Monkey Flower

Botanical Name	:	*Mimulus tigrinus*
Family	:	Scrophulariaceae
Common Name	:	Monkey Flower
Raising of Seedling	:	September-October
Transplanting Month	:	October-November
Planting Distance	:	30 cm x 30 cm
Height of Plant	:	Medium: 30-45 cm
Flowering Month	:	February-March
Colours	:	Bright yellowish, pink, crimson, red and marked with brown spots
Soil	:	Medium
Sunlight	:	Partial Shade
Irrigation	:	Heavy
Suitable For	:	Beddings and pots

All the flowers of all the tomorrows
are in the seeds of today.
Indian Proverb

The yellow flowers of *Mimulus tigrinus* have brown coloured irregular spots. They are large, tubular and two-tipped with open mouth and resemble a monkey face, hence called Monkey Flower. The annular branches have heart-shaped toothed leaves.

The plant is free-flowering and takes about 90-100 days to bloom. The plant does not flourish in warm weather, therefore its growth is generally confined to the northern hills. A light irrigation is preferred to a heavy dose.

Mimulus tigrinus is neither popular as cut or dry flower.

The flower has a peculiar look with multiple colour patterns which stand out well when sown in contrast with green foliage.

Bells of Ireland

Botanical Name	:	*Molucella laevis*
Family	:	Labiatae
Common Name	:	Bells of Ireland
Raising of Seedling	:	September-October
Transplanting Month	:	October-November
Planting Distance	:	30 cm x 30 cm
Height of Plant	:	Tall: 60-90 cm
Flowering Month	:	March-April
Colours	:	Green and foliage with non-conspicuous bluish flower
Soil	:	Heavy
Sunlight	:	Full
Irrigation	:	Normal
Suitable For	:	Beddings, as cut flowers and dried inflorescence for winter decoration

The flower is the poetry of reproduction.
It is an example of the eternal seductiveness of life.
Jean Giraudoux

Molucella paevis is a tall, hardy, free-flowering annual. The calyxes in the axial are bell-shaped, fascinating and persistent. A double-lipped inconspicuous small flower is engaged in it. The calyxes are green in colour and resemble bells which on maturity turn ivory white in colour. The leaves are star-shaped and the plant bears single and double flowers.

The plant thrives best in cool conditions and therefore requires long winters and needs cover from afternoon sun. The flowers appear in 120 days.

Bells of Ireland is an unpopular flower in home garden with elegant looks when green and dried. It is cultivated for making cut and dry floral designs. It is ideally suited for making 'lines' in geometric and in Ikebana style while used as fillers in bigger arrangements. The dry stem retains its lustre and strength up to a month. Bells of Ireland have a cut life of 7-10 days and are grown for their green effect in mixed flower beds, as dried and cut flowers. Chemically treated cut flowers last even up to a year which look equally fresh.

Nemesia

Botanical Name	:	*Nemesia strumosa*
Family	:	Scrophulariaceae
Common Name	:	Nemesia
Raising of Seedling	:	September-October
Transplanting Month	:	October-November
Planting Distance	:	15 cm x 15 cm
Height of Plant	:	Medium: 30-45 cm
Flowering Month	:	February-March
Colours	:	Yellow, orange, crimson, white, and marked with contrasting colours
Soil	:	Medium
Sunlight	:	Full but can also grow in shade
Irrigation	:	Normal
Suitable For	:	Beddings, borders and pot flowers

Flowers have spoken to me more than I can tell in written words.
They are the hieroglyphics of angels, loved by all men for the beauty of their character,
though few can decipher even fragments of their meaning.
Lydia M. Child

Nemesia strumosa is semi-hardy, bushy and compact in composition with erect branches. The leaves are oblong in shape. The plant is free-flowering with attractive, two-lipped flowers which are borne in clusters on the long stalk. The plant comes in both dwarf and tall varieties.

The seeds take 6-8 days to germinate and are then transplanted in the flower beds. The compact cluster of flowers at the top makes it an ideal choice as a pot flower. The flowers appear in about 90-100 days and a single flower remains open for 14 days.

Nemesia is used as a cut flower. A variety of colours and range of marking on the flowers makes the flower very popular.

Love-in-a-Mist

Botanical Name	:	*Nigella domascena*
Family	:	Ranunculaceae
Common Name	:	Love-in-a-Mist/Fennel Flower
Raising of Seedling	:	September-October
Transplanting Month	:	October-November
Planting Distance	:	30 cm x 30 cm
Height of Plant	:	Medium: 30-45 cm
Flowering Month	:	March-April
Colours	:	Varied colours
Soil	:	Medium
Sunlight	:	Full/Shady
Irrigation	:	Normal
Suitable For	:	Beddings, pot flowers, and as cut and dry flower

Who that had loved knows not the tender tail
which flowers reveal, when lips are coy to tell?
Edward George Earle Lytton Bulwar

Nigella domascena is a hardy annual with erect growth habits. It has finely cut, thread-like dark green feathery light foliage attached to the erect branches. The flowers are round and semi-double, almost 3-4 cm in diameter.

The plant does not stand transplanting well, thus seeds are sown direct at sight and thinned later. A little lime, rich and well-drained soil supports this charming and easily growing annual. Flowering commences within 80-100 days. It is a long day plant for vegetative growth and flowering.

The ornamental looking capsule (seed pods) decorates the flower arrangement. It is much admired as a dried flower.

Corn Poppy

Botanical Name	:	*Papaver rhoeas*
Family	:	Papaveraceae
Common Name	:	Corn Poppy
Raising of Seedling	:	September-October
Transplanting Month	:	October-November
Planting Distance	:	30 cm x 30 cm
Height of Plant	:	Tall: 60-90 cm
Flowering Month	:	February-April
Colours	:	Red, pink, scarlet, white and yellow
Soil	:	Light
Sunlight	:	Full
Irrigation	:	Mild
Suitable For	:	Beddings and borders

Summer set lip to earth's bosom bare,
And left the flushed print in a poppy there.
Francis Thompson – *The Poppy*

Papaver rhoeas is erect, branched and lobed with pinnatisect touched leaves. The flower, single or double, is saucer-shaped with silken petals. The flowers are borne on the elegantly shaped foliage with contrasting colour on edges and are sometimes edged or marked with flakes. The soft petals encircle the black centre. The fruit is of the shape of an ovoid capsule.

The plant is a weed of European cornfield but makes an elegant flower in the garden. Direct sowing is always preferred as the plant cannot withstand transplantation. The plant is perennial but considered as annual which blooms within 60-80 days. The annual poppies are almost foolproof to grow.

Profusion flowering compensates for the short-lived bloom. To stretch the blooming phase, continuously remove the seedpods.

An overdose of nitrogenous fertilizers yields a poor bloom. Opium is produced from the extract of the annual *P. somniferum* (Opium Poppy).

The bloom is followed by large and gloucous seedpods generally used for dry decorations which are cut along the stem.

The flowers are eye-catching, bright in colour, showy but worth keeping despite having a short lifespan.

Geranium

Botanical Name	:	*Pelargonium zonale*
Family	:	Geraniaceae
Common Name	:	Geranium
Raising of Seedling	:	August-September
Transplanting Month	:	September-November
Planting Distance	:	30 cm x 30 cm
Height of Plant	:	45 cm
Flowering Month	:	November-April
Colours	:	Pink, magenta, red, vermilion, white and peach
Soil	:	Medium
Sunlight	:	Full/Partial
Irrigation	:	Normal drainage
Suitable For	:	Beddings, window boxes and pot plants

Flowers are love's truest language.
P. Benjamin

Pelargonium zonale is an evergreen shruby perennial. Its flowers are borne in bundles.

Take the cutting of young, non-flowered sturdy shoots 5-6 cm in length and cleanly cut them beneath the node. Remove all the leaves and allow drying the cut surface. Insert the cuttings singly in pots or a dozen can be collectively inserted in bigger pots with good proportion of sand to ensure proper drainage. The cuttings should be kept moist and away from direct sunlight. After a few days when the cuttings have rooted transplant them into small pots containing two parts of garden soil, one part of sand and one part of well-rotten farmyard manure. A small dose of super phosphate will yield better results. Pinching the growing tip causes formation of new shoots and makes the plant bushy. Light irrigation and full sunlight during bloom is essential. As soon the flower buds appear, weekly application of liquid manure helps enrich the colour of the flowers. In the northern hills they bloom profusely throughout the summer while in the plains of North India, these add colour to the garden from December till hot summer winds start blowing.

The flowers are well known for their bright colour and beauty.

Petunia

Botanical Name	:	*Petunia hybrida*
Family	:	Solanaceae
Common Name	:	Petunia
Raising of Seedling	:	October
Transplanting Month	:	October-November
Planting Distance	:	45 cm x 30 cm
Height of Plant	:	Medium: 30-45 cm
Flowering Month	:	February-April
Colours	:	White, cream, purple, red, pink, blue, violet and mauve
Soil	:	Medium
Sunlight	:	Full
Irrigation	:	Moderate
Suitable For	:	Bedding, edging, mass effect, pots, hanging baskets and vase decorations

I have loved flowers that fade, within those magic tents
Rich hues have marriage made with sweet unmemoried scents.
Robert Seymour Bridges – *Shorter Poets*

Petunia hybrida is a sprawling, vigorously growing half-hardy showy annual. The leaves are soft, round, sticky, thick and small in size. The flower has five attractively veined petals joined together at the mouth to form a trumpet shape. The petals of single flowers are irregularly shaped while in the double flowers they are modified stamens into petals.

A cool weather is favourable for germination; therefore, delay sowing of the nursery by few days till appropriate weather conditions. Once the seedlings grow they are transplanted on site and the plant flowers in 90-100 days. Small and weak looking seedlings generally produce colourful bloom. The plant flourishes as the weather gets warm. It requires a well-drained rich soil with normal irrigation. Pinching is done to make the plant bushy. Plucking of faded flowers stretches the flowering period. To have a second bloom, cut the longest stem 1-2 inches above the ground after the first bloom and apply fertilizers or liquid manure. When the sepals are still green, light brown pods are collected between end-April to May. Buds are collected regularly and dried under shade. On drying the buds crack after 3-4 days and the seeds come out.

The plant is widely crossed and classified into various types. The appearance shows a wide diversification in many of its hybrid varieties. Petunia has lots of varieties and it becomes difficult to identify and select. The hybrid varieties are more prevalent.

It is a showy plant which is most useful for hanging baskets. Because of its long blooming period its flowers can be enjoyed till late season.

Phlox

Botanical Name	:	*Phlox drummondii*
Family	:	Polemoniaceae
Common Name	:	Phlox/Star Flower
Raising of Seedling	:	September-October
Transplanting Month	:	October-November
Planting Distance	:	30 cm x 30 cm
Height of Plant	:	Medium: 30-45 cm
Flowering Month	:	February-April
Colours	:	Shades of white, cream, red, pink and violet
Soil	:	Medium
Sunlight	:	Full
Irrigation	:	Normal
Suitable For	:	Bedding, borders, pot-flowers. Dwarf varieties are recommended for edging, window baskets and cut flowers

Every flower is a soul blossoming in Nature.
Gerard De Nerval

Phlox drummondii is bushy and erect in habit, thinly granular, heavy stemmed and covered with inconspicuous hairs. The leaves are entire, thin, narrow and pointed towards the tip. The flowers are 2-3 cm in diameter and are formed in clusters at the end of the branches to form a canopy. The new flower appears at the tip of the branches while later flowers appear from the axils of the leaves.

Numerous varieties are available in large and small flowers varying from separate to mix colours. Phlox is a favourite plant of gardeners and widely grown as it is easy to cultivate. The plant is free-flowering in habit with prolong flowering period. The plant needs rich and well-drained soil and thrives best in dry and cool climate. Pinching of the central shoot produces side branches making the plant bushy. It blooms within 90-110 days and a light dose of fertilizer prior to blooming yields quality flowers. Remove the entire bunch once the first bloom is over to reap another flush of bloom. To harvest seeds continue watering till May and then cut the stem and collect the seeds. March-April is the sowing period in hilly areas.

Phlox is a scented flower and gives a rich mass effect in the garden.

Lady's Lace

Botanical Name	:	*Ammi majus*
Family	:	Umbelliferae
Common Name	:	Lady's Lace
Raising of Seedling	:	September-October
Transplanting Month	:	October-November
Planting Distance	:	30 cm x 45 cm
Height of Plant	:	Tall: 90-120 cm
Flowering Month	:	January-March
Colours	:	White
Soil	:	Heavy
Sunlight	:	Full/Partial Shade
Irrigation	:	Normal
Suitable For	:	Bedding, background, as cut flowers and for dry decoration

Flowers grow out of dark moments.
Corita Kent

Pimpinella monoica has a long, slender, well-branched stem with deeply-cut green foliage. The white tiny flowers are produced in umbels and are placed in a loose spray fashion at the end of the branches. The flowers are either self-coloured or with contrasting colours formed in a mass.

Flowering starts late by mid-March and continues to bloom till the end of April. The plant grows well in rich and moist soil. Lady's Lace gives a good effect when sown against herbaceous shrub.

It is best grown as a cut flower and arranged in various floral designs. The faded flowers shed when kept for long duration indoors. The dried flowers are extensively used in dry flower arrangements.

Its usage as fresh flower is mostly in flower arrangements than in gardens.

Scarlet Sage

Botanical Name	:	*Salvia splendens*
Family	:	Labiatae
Common Name	:	Scarlet Sage
Raising of Seedling	:	September-October
Transplanting Month	:	October-November
Planting Distance	:	45 cm x 45 cm
Height of Plant	:	Tall: 60-90 cm
Flowering Month	:	February-April
Colours	:	Scarlet, red, purple, pink and shades of blue
Soil	:	Light to Medium
Sunlight	:	Full/Partial Shade
Irrigation	:	Normal
Suitable For	:	Beds, borders, background, pots and shrubs

As the gardener, such is the garden.
Hebrew Proverb

Salvia splendens is a hardy plant, bushy in composition with erect growth and wide range of size. It has dense foliage, broad heart-shaped glossy leaves having pointed ends and white hair underside. The flowers are borne above the foliage on long terminal spikes 15-25 cm in length which are thick, tubular and elongated at the tip.

The plant requires protection from frost, therefore must be sown under shady location and protected from the north and west direction. Pinching at an early stage makes the plant compact and bushy. Blooming after 90-100 days gives a gorgeous effect when sown against evergreen plantation. Continuous removal of dead spikes forms fresh branches and flowers. A regular dose of fertilizer is beneficial but an over-dose of nitrogenous fertilizer yields poor results. Seeds are sown in March-April and September-October in the northern hills, while in moderate climate of South they are sown in June where it is possible to reap a second flush when the plants are cut back.

The striking beautiful flowers are best suitable for areas with partial sunlight. Many varieties are available in different sizes and colours.

Cineraria

Botanical Name	:	*Senecio cruentus*
Family	:	Compositae
Common Name	:	Cineraria
Raising of Seedling	:	September-October
Transplanting Month	:	October-November
Planting Distance	:	30 cm x 30 cm
Height of Plant	:	Medium: 45 cm
Flowering Month	:	February-March
Colours	:	White, blue, purple, pink, lavender and scarlet
Soil	:	Medium
Sunlight	:	Full/Partial
Irrigation	:	Normal
Suitable For	:	Beddings, pots and as cut flowers

Beauty, unaccompanied by virtue, is as a flower without perfume.
French Proverb

Senecio cruentus is a medium size bushy annual having large heart-shaped velvety leaves. The flowers are compact, daisy-like or star-shaped. They are of brilliant colours and appear in clusters at the top of the branches. They may be marked with matching or contrasting white centre lending them an attractive look.

The minute seeds are mixed with equal quantity of sand and then broadcast in the nursery beds. Propagation multiplication is also done by stem cutting and division of old plant and roots. While preparing the nursery medium, add a small quantity of sand, leaf mould and little wood ash in the soil. Seedlings are picked when the first leaf appear and later transferred into flower beds at four leaf stages. Shade from strong sunlight and wind is essential for the plant. Cineraria thrives on long winters but also needs care from frost. It grows well in shade but three to four hours of sunshine is essential for this slow growing plant. When the buds start appearing, a mild dose of liquid manure improves the quality of the flowers. It is grown in March-April in the northern hills where a second bloom can be achieved by cutting down the stem to 3-4 cm from the surface followed by a top dressing.

Cineraria grows best in shady locations and is best suited for pot cultivation.

African Marigold

Botanical Name	:	*Tagetes erecta*
Family	:	Compositae
Common Name	:	African Marigold
Raising of Seedling	:	July-October
Transplanting Month	:	October-November
Planting Distance	:	45 cm x 30 cm
Height of Plant	:	Dwarf-Tall: 15-90 cm
Flowering Month	:	November-April
Colours	:	Orange, yellow and white
Soil	:	Heavy
Sunlight	:	Full
Irrigation	:	Normal
Suitable For	:	Beddings and as cut flowers

As for marigolds, poppies, hollyhocks, and valorous sunflowers,
we shall never have a garden without them, both for their own sake,
and for the sake of old-fashioned folks, who used to love them.
Henry Ward Beecher, *Star Papers* – 'A Discourse of Flowers'

The plant is very hardy, bushy and quick growing perennial which is treated as an annual. The leaves are dark in colour and deeply cut. The flowers have a variable diameter and are available in different forms.

Tagetes erecta is a popular countryside flower which flourishes in well-drained, rich, any type of soil in all seasons except in severe winters. The plant is tall in height bearing large flowers. Now a days, hybrid varities are preferred than open pollinated. Pinching is done to make the plant bushy and for better bloom. Avoid manure or fertilizers in excess as they only add foliage and not bloom. The plant is less prone to diseases but black spots on leaves, buds and flowers, leaf spots and leaf blight affect the plants. Apply Dithane M-45/Indofil M-45 @ 2 gram/litre and Rovral @ 2 grams/litre.

The flowers rarely fixed in fresh arrangements and are not used as dry flower.

Tagetes erecta is a flower for pots and garlands, and is also used as loose flower. It is known for its mass effect. However, some people may not admire its odour.

French Marigold

Botanical Name	:	*Tagetes patula*
Family	:	Compositae
Common Name	:	French Marigold
Raising of Seedling	:	June-November
Transplanting Month	:	October-November
Planting Distance	:	30 cm x 15 cm
Height of Plant	:	Medium: 30-45 cm
Flowering Month	:	October-April
Colours	:	Orange, yellow, burgundy and mixed shades
Soil	:	Heavy
Sunlight	:	Full
Irrigation	:	Normal
Suitable For	:	Flower beds, edge plants and rockery

The flowers are nature's jewels,
in whose wealth she decks her summer beauty.
Croly

Same as *Tagetes erecta* except *Tagetes patula* is
dwarf with small flowers in different colours. They
are essentially bedding marigold. The tall growing
varieties are grown for loose flower production.

Nasturtium

Botanical Name	:	*Tropaeolum majus/minor*
Family	:	Tropaeolaceae
Common Name	:	Nasturtium
Raising of Seedling	:	September-October
Transplanting Month	:	October-November
Planting Distance	:	30 cm x 30 cm
Height of Plant	:	Medium: 30-45 cm
Flowering Month	:	February-March
Colours	:	Red, orange, yellow, scarlet and various hues
Soil	:	Light
Sunlight	:	Full/Partial
Irrigation	:	Mild
Suitable For	:	Beddings, ground cover, border plants, hanging baskets and as pot flowers

*Art is the unceasing effort to compete with the beauty of flowers –
and never succeeding.*
Marc Chagall

Tropaeolum majus have smooth, wiry and sprawling stems. The leaves are round and green in colour while few varieties have spots and markings. The large spurred flower consists of five petals with sepals of spur-like end.

Nasturtium is very commonly sown as it is easy to grow and flourishes on any kind of soil. Direct sowing is always preferred. The flowers are single or double and require at least half-day sunlight. The flowering takes place within 80-90 days. There are few varieties; the dwarf variety is suitable for pots and flower beds while the tall ones can be trained as climbers; a few are also creeping in nature. A light irrigation and restrained manure produces less foliage and boosts the bloom. Any excessive foliage can be thinned manually. Main varieties are floriferous and they are available in a wide range of colour.

The decorative leaves and flowers are fabulous in flower arrangements. It is grown for its unusual shape. It is included in edible flower list and its leaves are also used as tossed salad in Europe.

Verbena

Botanical Name	:	*Verbena hybrida*
Family	:	Verbenaceae
Common Name	:	Verbena
Raising of Seedling	:	September-October
Transplanting Month	:	October-November
Planting Distance	:	30 cm x 30 cm
Height of Plant	:	Dwarf: 30-40 cm
Flowering Month	:	February-March
Colours	:	Blue, white, pink, purple, red, lavender and in exquisite range of colours
Soil	:	Light
Sunlight	:	Full
Irrigation	:	Normal
Suitable For	:	Raised beds, edging, rockery, pots, hanging baskets and window boxes

Earth laughs in flowers.
Ralph Waldo Emerson

Verbena hybrida is half-hardy, trailing in habit and a free-flowering annual. The leaves are small in size, wrinkled and deeply cut. The clusters of flowers are groups of small tubes attached to the five petals resembling a star formation. The flowers are formed in loose clusters above the foliage on the short stem.

The plant is early flowering and suitable for ground cover under tall plants. A mild irrigation is desirable to harvest a good bloom. Pinching makes the growth bushy. Early forming buds must be removed to get compact growth for covering the top. A top dressing thoroughly mixed with soil is beneficial. The bloom is completed by May-June and seeds can be collected thereafter. In areas with moderate temperature and low rainfall, seeds are sown in April and September.

The sweet scented flower with vivid colours and spots gives a spectacular effect for a long duration.

Pansy

Botanical Name	:	*Viola tricolor (Wittro ckina)*
Family	:	Violaceae
Common Name	:	Pansy
Raising of Seedling	:	September-October
Transplanting Month	:	October-November
Planting Distance	:	15 cm x 15 cm
Height of Plant	:	Dwarf: 20-30 cm
Flowering Month	:	February-April
Colours	:	White, yellow, blue, violet, red and different colours with or without blotch
Soil	:	Medium
Sunlight	:	Full/Partial
Irrigation	:	Normal
Suitable For	:	Beddings, edging, borders, window boxes, hanging baskets and pot plants. It is an ideal combination when sown as ground cover with roses and bulbs

*I know not which I love the most, nor which the comeliest shows, the timid,
bashful violet or the royal-hearted rose; The pansy in purple dress, the pink with cheek of red,
or the faint, fair heliotrope, who hangs, Like a bashful maid her head.*
Phoebe Cary – *Spring Flowers*

Viola tricolor is dwarf in size, bushy in growth and trailing in habit. The heart shape leaves bear cuts at equal distance along the borders. The magnificent flowers on elongated stalks have peculiar butterfly shape with fascinating, eye-catching colours, markings and combinations.

A perennial in plains and biennial in hills, it requires rich, well-cultivated and well-drained soil. Hybrid varieties are preferred to open pollinated. Cover the seedlings during the early phase from excessive heat and transplant them after four weeks. A light dose of liquid manure during flowering is suggested. The flower appears after 110-120 days. The small varieties produce flowers 3-4 cm in size in great profusion which gives a good mass effect in flower beds. The large variety flowers are 6-9 cm in size, showy and more suitable for pots. Single bud on each shoot produces flowers of exceptional beauty.

The flowers only with long stem are used as cut flowers which have a cut life of 3-4 days.

Pansy is admired for its shape, colourful flowers and sweet scent. It makes an excellent pot plant for exhibition and flower shows.

Teen-Patia

Botanical Name	:	*Amaranthus tricolor*
Family	:	Amarantaceae
Common Name	:	Teen-Patia
Raising of Seedling	:	February-March
Transplanting Month	:	April-May
Planting Distance	:	30 cm x 30 cm
Height of Plant	:	Tall: 90-120 cm
Flowering Month	:	May-June
Colours	:	Crimson and greenish-white flowers
Soil	:	Medium
Sunlight	:	Full
Irrigation	:	Heavy
Suitable For	:	Pots, beddings and foliage for flower arrangements as independent identity. They are not grouped with flowers as the foliage will dominate the flowers

Men do not weigh the stalk for that it was,
When once they find her flower, her glory, pass.
Samuel Daniel

Amaranthus tricolour is a tall hardy annual with vigorous growth. The leaves are simple green in colour when young which change their colour and develop marking or form variegated leaves. The plant is free-flowering in habit and produces drooping tails of tiny flowers.

It has many species with ornamental value consisting foliage and bloom or both. Some species are trailing while a few bear tiny flowers. A rich soil, moisture and sunny location combine to form luxurious foliage as in poor soil the foliage does not grow well and in locations with partial shade the colours do not fully develop. The plantation in rainy season yields best results. A light dose of liquid manure during the growth phase is beneficial. It is sown in February-March in hills and almost round-the-year in areas with mild climate where winters are not severe and dryness is less. It takes 80-90 days for the plant to grow to its full elegance.

The plant is grown for its colour, foliage and attractive spikes.

Coreopsis

Botanical Name	:	*Coreopsis tinctonia*
Family	:	Compositae
Common Name	:	Coreopsis
Raising of Seedling	:	February-March
Transplanting Month	:	April-May
Planting Distance	:	30 cm x 15 cm
Height of Plant	:	Tall: 60-90 cm
Flowering Month	:	June-July
Colours	:	Yellow with maroon centre
Soil	:	Medium
Sunlight	:	Full
Irrigation	:	Heavy
Suitable For	:	Beddings, screening and borders

To see a world in a Grain of Sand, And a Heaven in a Wild Flower,
Hold Infinity in the palm of your hand, And eternity in an hour.
William Blake

Coreopsis tinctonia has a tall stem and the single daisy-like flowers are 3-4 cm wide.

Coreopsis can be propagated with ease but it is not very commonly grown in home gardens. The plant gives a good mass effect when sown densely to give a compact look. It takes 60-80 days to bloom. Towards the end of flowering in the month of March, cut the plant stems 12-18 inch from the ground. Apply a dose of fertilizers and irrigate it frequently. Thereafter, the flowers will appear much faster than the first bloom.

Cosmos

Botanical Name	:	*Cosmos sulphureus*
Family	:	Compositae
Common Name	:	Cosmos
Raising of Seedling	:	February-March
Transplanting Month	:	April-May
Planting Distance	:	25 cm x 45 cm
Height of Plant	:	Tall: 60-90 cm
Flowering Month	:	May-June
Colours	:	Yellow, orange, ivory & brick red
Soil	:	Medium
Sunlight	:	Full
Irrigation	:	Heavy
Suitable For	:	Beddings and borders

Give me odorous at sunrise a garden of beautiful flowers
where I can walk undisturbed.
Walt Whitman

Cosmos sulphureus is tall in height having well-branched wiry stems. The leaves are long, thin, feathery and deeply cut. The central petals form a tuft-like cluster of the flower head while broad and long ray florets remain in the background.

Cosmos is a hardy, very robust plant which can be grown throughout the year in adverse, warm and humid conditions. Direct sowing always yields better results. Heavy dose of manure causes growth of foliage and curtails the growth of flowers. The texture of Cosmos is quite similar to Coreopsis. Flowers start appearing within 50-60 days. *C. sulphureus* is economical to grow and easy to maintain in comparison to *C. bipinnatus*.

The flower has a cut life of 4-5 days and can be used in tall arrangements.

Cosmos is a popular annual as it is easy to propagate and gives a good mass effect.

Blanket Flower

Botanical Name	:	*Gaillardia aristata*
Family	:	Compositae
Common Name	:	Blanket Flower
Raising of Seedling	:	February-March
Transplanting Month	:	April-May
Planting Distance	:	45 cm x 30 cm
Height of Plant	:	Medium: 45-60 cm
Flowering Month	:	May-October
Colours	:	Yellow, orange, crimson, brown, scarlet and mixed colours
Soil	:	Moderate
Sunlight	:	Full
Irrigation	:	Heavy
Suitable For	:	Beddings and as cut flowers

Flowers ... are a proud assertion that
a ray of beauty outvalues all the utilities of the world.
Ralph Waldo Emerson

The stem is thin and bears smooth, long leaves. The flowers consist of serrated petals encircling the dark colour centre.

Gaillardia aristata is perennial in hills and the hardiest annual on plains that can be grown in any soil and sown throughout the year in summers (February-March), rainy season (May-June) and in winters (September-October). Blooming takes place after 90-120 days which can be prolonged by regular withdrawal of faded flowers. The flower is ready to harvest when the ray florets drop and the head changes its colour to grey.

Gaillardia aristata is widely grown as it is easy to propagate, forms heavy mass effect and thick foliage.

Gomphrena

Botanical Name	:	*Gomphrena haageana*
Family	:	Amaranthaceae
Common Name	:	Gomphrena
Raising of Seedling	:	February-March; May-June
Transplanting Month	:	March-April; June-July
Planting Distance	:	30 cm x 30 cm
Height of Plant	:	Medium: 50-60 cm
Flowering Month	:	May-June; July-August
Colours	:	Purple, deep magenta, orange, pink and white
Soil	:	Light-Medium
Sunlight	:	Full
Irrigation	:	Normal
Suitable For	:	Beddings, borders and pots

The flowers of late winter and early spring occupy
places in our hearts well out of proportion to their size.
Gertrude S. Wister

Gomphrena haageana is bushy in composition having long, thin and strong stems. The leaves are narrow and long. The flower heads are papery in texture, round, button-shaped and 2-3 cm in diameter resembling a coat button.

It is a robust annual, easy to cultivate and with an extended flowering period. Flowering begins 60-80 days after transplanting. To get an eye-catching effect propagate multiple colour varieties. In the northern hills seeds are sown in March-April, while in South India in September-October.

The cut life of the flower head is about 7 days but for better results the stem needs to be cut daily from the base and water changed regularly. As the flower is small in size, it is considered for small size arrangements, bowls and for mass arrangements. The flower heads are cut with their long stem and dried. The flowers do not lose their colour, lustre and composition for a long time; therefore, they are also called everlasting flowers. Most common varieties of *Gomphrena globossa* are used in the market as loose, fresh and dry flowers.

Sunflower

Botanical Name	:	*Helianthus annus*
Family	:	Compositae
Common Name	:	Sunflower
Raising of Seedling	:	February-March
Transplanting Month	:	March-April
Planting Distance	:	45 cm x 30 cm
Height of Plant	:	Tall: 90-120 cm
Flowering Month	:	May-June
Colours	:	Yellow, orange and bronze
Soil	:	Medium
Sunlight	:	Full
Irrigation	:	Heavy
Suitable For	:	Borders, beddings, screens and as cut flowers

The Sun flower blushed to own the nameless flower as her kin,
The sun rose and smiled on it saying, 'Are you well my darling'.
Rabindranath Tagore

Helianthus annus is a tall, hardy annual with vigorous growth. It has a tough herbaceous stem with rough textured leaves bearing flower heads at the tip of the side branches. The large flower heads consist of a number of discs and ray florets.

The flower head must be sown in a sunny location as it follows the course of the sun. The tall size plants require well-cultivated soil to accommodate the deep roots. A fully grown plant requires staking. Due to its tall height it does not go well along with other flowering annuals and hence should be grown as an independent identity. The seeds can also be sown directly or in nursery beds, where they take 4-6 days to germinate and later transplanted in the flower beds. The plant takes 100-120 days to blossom. Ornamental varieties are not used for oil extradiction. In South India where the climate is mild it can be sown round the year, i.e., April-September-January.

The decorative flowers with long stems are good as cut flowers and can be used for heavy flower arrangements.

The sparkling sun-shaped yellow colour flower makes it attractive and adorable.

Kochia

Botanical Name	:	*Kochia scoparia*
Family	:	Chenopodiaceae
Common Name	:	Kochia
Raising of Seedling	:	February-April
Transplanting Month	:	March-May
Planting Distance	:	45 cm x 45 cm or 60 cm x 60 cm
Height of Plant	:	Tall: 60-75 cm
Flowering Month	:	May-August
Colours	:	Pale green
Soil	:	Heavy
Sunlight	:	Full/Partial
Irrigation	:	Heavy
Suitable For	:	Borders, pots, along pavements and for making temporary screens

*When you have only two pennies left in the world,
buy a loaf of bread with one, and a lily with the other.*
Chinese Proverb

Kochia scoparia is a dense, bushy plant having an oval shape. The finely cut, pale-green, fluffy leaves form a tuft of lush green foliage during the peak summer season.

It takes 80-100 days to grow up to full size. The foliage beauty is at zenith when the plant is about 45 cm in height. The foliage turns copper-red towards the end of the life and subsequently the red flower appears which later produces seeds. One plant in a 20-25 cm pot gives good outlook.

The plant is exploited for its formal oval shape, lush green foliage and long vegetative life. It is best suitable for children parks because of its tender nature of foliage.

Sun Plant

Botanical Name	:	*Portulaca grandiflora*
Family	:	Portulaceae
Common Name	:	Sun Plant/Moss Rose
Raising of Seedling	:	March-April
Transplanting Month	:	April-May
Planting Distance	:	15 cm x 15 cm
Height of Plant	:	Dwarf: 15-20 cm
Flowering Month	:	May-September
Colours	:	Orange, purple, red, pink, yellow and white
Soil	:	Light
Sunlight	:	Full
Irrigation	:	Normal
Suitable For	:	Sunny spots, edging, hanging baskets, shallow pots, carpet beddings and ground cover

Portulaca grandiflora has round and short fleshy stems bearing cup-shaped single or double flowers. The leaves are cylindrical, thick, fleshy and pointed.

The plant is pretty, low-growing hardy with creeping habit and requires less propagation care. It is easy to grow and requires moist sandy soil. Dryness and dampness is injurious to the plant. The very minute seeds are mixed with sand for uniform spread and sown in nursery beds or flower beds. It takes 8-10 days for the seeds to germinate and flowering takes place in 90-110 days. Perennial varieties are multiplied by top cuttings.

The flowers open in the morning under full sunshine and close by afternoon or immediately when kept under shade. It flourishes best in summers and rainy season and can grow throughout the year in moderate climate but cannot withstand extreme cold.

The plant is compactly sown and admired for its mass effect.

Zinnia

Botanical Name	:	*Zinnia elegans*
Family	:	Compositae
Common Name	:	Zinnia
Raising of Seedling	:	June-July
Transplanting Month	:	July-August
Planting Distance	:	45 cm x 45 cm or 60 cm x 60 cm
Height of Plant	:	Dwarf: below 30 cm to Tall: 30-90 cm
Flowering Month	:	September-November
Colours	:	White, yellow, crimson, red, orange, salmon, mauve and purple
Soil	:	Medium
Sunlight	:	Full
Irrigation	:	Heavy
Suitable For	:	Beds, borders, pots and as cut flowers

I wandered lonely as a cloud. That floats on high o'er vales and hills,
When all at once I saw a crowd, A host, of golden daffodils;
Beside the lake beneath the trees, Fluttering and dancing in the breeze.
William Wordsworth

Zinnia elegans is erect in habit and neat in outlook having few branches. The rough leaves are simple and oblong with rounded tips. The beautiful flower heads are round in form and are borne at the top of the branches. They consist of disc and ray florets which are flat-quelled and ruffled. The flowers are single, semi-double and double.

There are numerous vigorously growing, easy-to-cultivate, dwarf to tall varieties. Zinnia can be grown throughout the year under favourable conditions. In South India these can be grown in the months of April, September and January while in the northern hills the seeds are sown in March-April. In the plains of North India best results are seen when sown in rich soil at sunny location during the summer season. After 40-50 days of sowing, when the flower buds start appearing, pinching must be done to make the plant bushy and to avoid formation of inferior quality flowers. A top dressing at bud formation stage produces quality flowers. The top heavy plants may also require staking.

Pompon-shaped flowers of Zinnia extensively form an integral part in floral designs. The stem needs a long drink prior to fixing in arrangements. Zinnia's mass effect is graceful.

Love Lies Bleeding

Botanical Name	:	*Amaranthus caudatus*
Family	:	Amarantaceae
Common Name	:	Love Lies Bleeding
Raising of Seedling	:	May-June
Transplanting Month	:	July-August
Planting Distance	:	30 cm x 30 cm
Height of Plant	:	Tall: 60-90 cm
Flowering Month	:	August-September
Colours	:	Pink and white
Soil	:	Medium
Sunlight	:	Full
Irrigation	:	Normal
Suitable For	:	Beddings and pots

*Who would have thought it possible that
a tiny little flower could preoccupy a person so completely that
there simply wasn't room for any other thought.*
Sophie Scholl

Amaranthus caudatus is a tall hardy annual with vigorous growth. The leaves are simple green in colour when young which change their colour and develop marking or form variegated leaves. The plant is free-flowering in habit and produces drooping tails of tiny flowers.

It has many species with ornamental value consisting foliage and bloom or both. Some species are trailing while a few bear tiny flowers. A rich soil, moisture and sunny location combine to form luxurious foliage as in poor soil the foliage does not grow well and in semi-shade locations the colour does not fully develop. The plantation yields best results in rainy season. A light dose of liquid manure during the growth period is beneficial. It is sown in February-March in hills and almost round-the-year in areas with mild climate where winters are not severe and dryness is less. It takes about 80-90 days for the plant to grow to its full elegance.

The plant is grown for its colour foliage and attractive spikes.

Mexican Sunflower

Botanical Name	:	*Tithonia rotundifolia*
Family	:	Compositae
Common Name	:	Mexican Sunflower
Raising of Seedling	:	April-May; August-September
Transplanting Month	:	July-August; October-November
Planting Distance	:	60 cm x 60 cm
Height of Plant	:	Tall: 120-180 cm
Flowering Month	:	August-September; February-March
Colours	:	Yellow and orange-red
Soil	:	Light
Sunlight	:	Full
Irrigation	:	Normal
Suitable For	:	Beddings, borders, hedges, screening, shrubs and as cut flowers

*There is something remarkably more beautiful about flowers
that you yourself have planted, and divided, and cared for, than any other flowers.
It reminds one that the creation of beauty is a happy experience.*
Claudia Lady Bird Johnson

Tithonia rotundifolia is a tall, hardy, brittle stalked, free-flowering showy annual. The leaves are large, rough and heart-shaped. The single large orange-red flower with tufted yellow centre resembles the single Dahlia. Flowers are borne on the long stalk, 8-10 cm in size where the single petals are grouped around the yellow centres.

Tithonia rotundifolia has its origin in Mexico and therefore known as Mexican Sunflower. A well manured light soil with little care brings the flowers in profusion within 90 days.

The flowers are widely used as cut flowers and are most suitable for screening.

Mexican Sunflower is popular for its mass effect.

Celosia

Botanical Name	:	*Celosia argentea var. plumosa*
Family	:	Amarantaceae
Common Name	:	Celosia
Raising of Seedling	:	April-May
Transplanting Month	:	May-June
Planting Distance	:	45 cm x 45 cm
Height of Plant	:	Intermediate: 45-60 cm
Flowering Month	:	July-August
Colours	:	Crimson, red, orange, maroon and golden
Soil	:	Medium
Sunlight	:	Full
Irrigation	:	Normal
Suitable For	:	Beddings, pots and as cut flowers

Flowers are words,
which even a babe may understand.
Bishop Arthur Cleveland Coxe – *The Singing of Birds*

Celosia plumosa bears simple leaves having variation in colour and fleshy stems with storage space. The plant produces long, feathery flower heads on large plumes of elongated pyramidal shape.

Seeds may be sown direct in the flower beds and take about 7-10 days to germinate. It takes 70-75 days for the plant to flower. The propagation practices are same as *Var. cristata*.

It is often used as cut flower and dried flower. It is a common and much admired flower that grows in the rainy season.

Cockscomb

Botanical Name	:	*Celosia argentea var. cristata*
Family	:	Amarantaceae
Common Name	:	Cockscomb
Raising of Seedling	:	March-April
Transplanting Month	:	May-June
Planting Distance	:	30 cm x 30 cm
Height of Plant	:	Intermediate: 45-60 cm
Flowering Month	:	August-October
Colours	:	Maroon, yellow, crimson, purple and red
Soil	:	Medium
Sunlight	:	Full
Irrigation	:	Normal
Suitable For	:	Beddings, borders, hedges and as dried flowers

In my garden there is a large place for sentiment.
My garden of flowers is also my garden of thoughts and dreams.
The thoughts grow as freely as the flowers, and the dreams are as beautiful.
Abram L. Urban

The plant is very hardy with a long stem. The velvety texture bears feathery flower heads formed above the foliage which resemble cockscomb from which it derives its common name.

A very popular annual, it forms a spectacular appearance. The seedlings are transplanted quite young to avoid transplantation shock. The plant takes 90 days to flower and thereafter has a long flowering period. During the rainy season the plant is often attacked by fungal diseases and pests. It is advisable to keep only good quality flower heads and uproot the others. A dose of liquid manure is effective. When sown in pots, transfer only those plants which develop bigger flower heads for a better outlook.

It is a nice cut flower as it survives for 5-7 days and can also be preserved as dried flower as it retains its colour for a long period.

It is a popular and pretty rainy season flower.

Balsam Gulmendi

Botanical Name	:	*Impatiens balsamina*
Family	:	Balsaminaceae
Common Name	:	Balsam Gulmendi
Raising of Seedling	:	April-May
Transplanting Month	:	May-June
Planting Distance	:	30 cm x 30 cm
Height of Plant	:	Tall: 60-75 cm
Flowering Month	:	August-September
Colours	:	Orange, red, pink, mauve, cream, white and purplish-red
Soil	:	Heavy
Sunlight	:	Full
Irrigation	:	Normal
Suitable For	:	Beddings, borders and as pot flowers

To cultivate a Garden is to walk with God.
Bover

Impatiens balsamina is a tall plant with simple, thin, toothed margin leaves. The flowers are borne on the leaf axial.

The seeds are sown in nursery beds which germinate in 4-6 days; thereafter they are transplanted in the flower beds. Early sowing should be avoided as it results in excessive vegetative growth and lesser bloom. However, it is an early flowering rainy season plant. The plant cannot sustain dry conditions and flourishes in rich, moist soil. The side shoots should be removed regularly so that only the main shoot remains which produces large-sized flowers. Closely placed plants do not produce quality flowers. A dose of liquid manure is recommended fortnightly.

Flowers appear within 60-70 days after transplantation. The seeds are harvested in October when pods containing the seeds turn yellowish and become dry.

Sada Bahar

Botanical Name	:	*Vinca rosea*
Family	:	Apocynaceae
Common Name	:	Sada Bahar
Raising of Seedling	:	February-April
Transplanting Month	:	July-August
Planting Distance	:	30 cm x 30 cm
Height of Plant	:	Intermediate: 30-45 cm
Flowering Month	:	March-October
Colours	:	Purple or white. New varieties are available in attractive shades of pink and red with much larger flowers having a blotch in the centre
Soil	:	Light to heavy
Sunlight	:	Full/Partial
Irrigation	:	Mild
Suitable For	:	Beddings, rockeries, borders and pots

Many eyes go through the meadow, but few see the flowers in it.
Ralph Waldo Emerson

Vinca rosea is thinly branched and bushy at the top. The dark green leaves are small, smooth, polished, oblong, and rounded at the point. They are shining in appearance and distinctly veined. The five petals are connected to a thin tube and the flowers are with or without a reddish eye in the centre.

The plant is a herbaceous perennial treated as an annual. It can be easily propagated sowing of seeds or cuttings at any time of the year in any kind of soil and can withstand both warm and drought climatic conditions. Extreme winters affect the flowering but once established the plant flowers throughout the year. Rich soil and good irrigation makes the plant bushy with good yield of flowering. The plant must be cut back/headed back every four-six months and replaced every two year. It is rarely attacked by any pest and diseases.

The leaves are considered good for diabetic people.

Nursery Raising and Transplantation

Raising the Nursery

Most of the seasonal flowers are grown from seeds and a selected few by vegetative methods. A nursery is raised for better handling of delicate and minute seeds in a small area. The process involves procurement of seeds, preparation of nursery medium and sowing of seeds. Procurement of seeds requires complete knowledge and thorough survey because all efforts thereafter are futile if sub-standard seeds are sown. Prefer buying known varieties of seeds having longer duration of flowering from reliable sources. These days, reputed seed companies supply seeds in sealed packaging having high germination percentage. The seeds are sown on raised beds enriched with well-decomposed FYM or leaf mould in the following composition:

- One part of soil
- One part of river sand
- One part of well-rotten farmyard manure
- One part of leaf mould or burnt rice husk

Thoroughly incorporate the following fertilizers in the upper layer of the nursery beds.

- 60 gram/sq m of CAN
- 60 gram/sq m of muriate of potash
- 120 gram/sq m of super phosphate

Prepare raised nursery beds 8-10 cm high and 24-36 cm wide with intermediate water channels so as to ensure that when the channels are filled with water they are able to completely wet the raised bed through seepage.

The nursery beds should be drenched with Captaf 0.2% to take care of soil-born diseases. The sterilization of nursery bed is also done by chemicals using Formaline 40%. Visit a pesticide shop for latest sterilizing agents. Wear gloves and use face-mask in order to avoid inhalation of chemical fumes. Prepare the mixture as per prescription. Drench the nursery medium, cover it with a polythene and then remove the sheet after a week. Thereafter, expose the soil mixture to the sun for another 3-4 days to remove the effect of the chemical.

When the soil becomes workable, it is ready for sowing. Seeds should be sown thinly and evenly to produce healthy seedlings. Some flower seeds, e.g. *Senecio cruentus* (Cineraria) are very light and tiny; even a slight breeze carries them away. They should be mixed with small quantity of sand and broadcast on the nursery bed. A fine layer of the soil mix is spread on the top just to cover the seeds thoroughly. In general, the seeds should be sown at a depth according to their size and covered with a very fine layer of leaf mould. Prefer to sow the seeds in lines. Sprinkle the nursery bed immediately with a light mist of water. To prevent ants from carrying away the seeds, Chloropyrifos 20 EC powder can be dusted along the borders of the nursery beds.

Cover the nursery bed with a newspaper, plastic sheet or 'sarkanda' to protect it from excessive heat and dehydration during hot weather and from frost during cold weather. In normal weather conditions cover it with a fine translucent fabric/material which will allow the light to pass through and retain moisture. To keep the nursery medium moist and soft, water the nursery bed when the surface shows signs of dryness. The wooden pans with seeds sown can be transferred to the 'germination area' where they are subjected to controlled light, temperature and humidity in order to provide required germination condition.

Generally, seeds germinate within two weeks and are ready for transplanting on attaining 7-10 cm height or once they have developed at least 3-4 leaves. The seedlings are hardened before transplanting by withholding watering for 1-2 days. Hardening of seedlings becomes essential for the seedlings which are raised under the protected environment of shade. The hardened seedlings withstand transplanting shock better than those which are not hard.

When the soil is still soft, loosen it near the base of the seedling using a narrow blade 'khurpa'. Hold the seedling with your fingers and gently pull it out from the nursery bed. Ensure that the soil around the delicate roots remains attached to them. Now immediately transfer the seedlings into the soil beds.

Ready-made 'sterilized plastic plug trays' of various plug sizes are available in the market. Sow the seed in each plug; the after-care procedure is same as discussed earlier. Once the seedlings are ready for transplantation, stop watering them and after 1-2 days, gently tap at the sides of the plug, take out the seedlings and transfer them into the flower beds. Seedlings in plugs ensure very high rate of establishment on transplantation. Earthen or wooden pans can also be prepared to germinate the seedlings, which are then transplanted into the flower bed. Remember to spread a layer of gravel at the bottom of the pans to prevent

blocking of the drainage holes. Ideally, earthen or wooden pans should be watered with a fine mist or by placing the pans in a container filled with water so that the water enters from the drainage hole.

Preparation of Flower Beds

While the nursery seedlings are growing, it is appropriate time to prepare the flower beds. To prepare soil beds, water the soil to loosen it and to make it workable. Thoroughly weed out all the existing vegetation in the flower bed. Normal width of the beds may vary from 2-4 feet which enables easy working of soil. Dig up the soil up to 15-20

cm deep; the soil lumps should be broken and exposed to the sun for at least 1-2 weeks. It is advisable to have pre-emptive protection against termites at the time of preparing the soil bed by drenching the soil bed with Chloropyrifos 20 EC (1 ml/liter) or use any other recommended pesticide. Apply six to seven baskets (or 5-6 kg) of well-decomposed farmyard manure and add super phosphate @ 750 grams and muriate of potash @ 500 grams in a hundred square meter area (10 X 10). Mix the ingredients thoroughly with a shovel and later with hand to make it into a fine medium for plant growth. As the root system in annuals does not develop beyond 20-30 cm, treatment to the soil should therefore not extend beyond this depth. Level the soil bed to make the water flow gradually and not allowing the nutrients be washed away to low-lying areas. The soil bed is now prepared and ready for transplantation.

Soil: The soil holds the plant and provides water and nutrition for its sustenance and development. Annuals have a short life-span and the active growth takes place within a period of about two-three months. They have limited time to stabilize

and flourish and, therefore, need fertile soil to develop their root system during their life-span. Therefore, management of the soil and fertility is very crucial. However, it is advantageous if the soil be analyzed both for its 'pH' and 'nutrient' levels which will help in management of the soil. Practically no soil is ideal; soils differ in physical and biological properties. It has to be developed and renewed periodically depending upon the usage. Loam soil with pH 6.5 to 7.5 enriched with well-rotten FYM could be considered best for growing seasonal flowers. However, many seasonal flowers can withstand soil with higher pH value up to 8.5.

Drainage: Good drainage is the most important factor for proper air-water relations in the soil and to sustain growth of the plants. Plants do not withstand standing water even for a short while and get into stress affecting their growth and development. Seasonal flowers do well in well-drained, loose soil enriched with organic manures. Drainage becomes a serious problem in the low-lying areas, and under excessive rainfall conditions. The excessive water on the surface is drained making surface drains 16-30 cm deep. Even if the top-soil is light and porous but the sub-soil constitute of clay/heavy, it still needs to be drained by making sub-soil drain.

Transplanting

If a firmly compressed soil readily crumbles apart on release of hand pressure it is suitable for sowing. Thereafter, seedlings should be transferred preferably in the evening hours to avoid strong sunlight followed by low temperature.

Moisten the nursery medium to ensure smooth withdrawal of seedlings. Then carefully scoop them from the bottom with the help of a weeding 'khurpi' and separate them gently without disturbing the soil from the roots. Seedlings are handled by their leaves and are not touched by their stem as they are quite

tender and may get damaged. A hole is made in proportion to the size of the root system at the specified distance, depending upon the potential height and spread of the plant. The seedling is now lowered and the soil medium is settled thoroughly to make complete contact with the root. Ensure that the root has slipped in completely straight without any bend.

Irrigation must be done immediately with the help of a fine low-pressure hose so that the seedlings are not uprooted. Allow water to trickle into the soil and firm the roots. If any seedling happens to fall, firm it with the help of soil. Review the transplantation next day. If any plant is dislocated or tilted due to the pressure of water, wind, weight of free-floating pieces of manure or loose grip of soil, support it adequately with soil. Subsequently, if some seedlings happen to die, replace them with fresh seedlings from the nursery bed. If the seeds are sown directly at site, select the most healthy and strong seedlings and remove the others. In direct sowing, thinning can be done in the second week when the seedlings have grown.

Care of Seedlings

The seedlings should be given light irrigation for about first three to five days till they are established. In summers, irrigate them in the evening so as to ensure the soil remains moist but avoid water-logging which is harmful for the seedlings. In winters, irrigate them in the afternoon. The frequency of irrigation can vary depending upon the requirement of the plant and weather conditions. Once the plants are established, approximately in a week's time, flood the soil bed with water. When the soil becomes workable, hoeing and weeding are done to make the soil porous and to uproot unwanted seedlings. Then the soil is exposed to the sun for 1-2 days. Keep the soil moist but not sodden as it will encourage tremendous foliage growth but scanty bloom. Nitrogenous fertilizers may also be applied in the beds at fortnightly interval at 15–20

gram per square meter or the liquid formulation of urea at 2 gram in 10 liters of water for per square meter of area.

When the seeds are sown directly in the soil in case of holly hock, sweet peas, etc. uproot the weak seedlings and those grown in double. Again, after two weeks, thin out the seedlings to maintain the recommended distance and fill the gaps by withdrawing the seedlings from places where grown in clusters.

Vegetative Propagation

Plants generally reproduce through seeds, but plants grown from seeds may not be identical with the parent. To ensure the raising of identical offspring another process is practiced in which a vegetative part of the plant is used for propagation. Hence it is known as 'vegetative reproduction' or 'asexual propagation'. This process is lengthy, time-consuming, and requires excessive care as well as expertise, but produces a true replica of the parent plant. However, continuous vegetative propagation deteriorates the quality of the stock. For vegetative propagation, the gardener must know: the proper time of the year which could be late winter for hard wood cutting and rainy season for soft and semi-hard wood cuttings. The other methods of vegetative propagation include cutting, budding, grafting, layering and division.

Cutting

It is a very popular and easy method of multiplying plants. A cutting of stem, leaf, is rooted into the medium under optimum conditions to form an identical new plant. Cutting can be of various types as mentioned below.

Stem Cutting

Soft Wood Cutting: Among the seasonal flowers, Chrysanthemum, Petunia, Dahlia, Marigold, Salvia,

Lupin and Coleus are multiplied by this method. There are many herbaceous shrubs, climbers and perennials that are also propagated by this method.

Methodology: A 7-10 cm long terminal cutting is taken from plants with 4-5 leaves intact for rooting in the sand. If the length of the cutting is more, cut it from the basal side to bring it to the prescribed size. Except 2-3 terminal leaves remove all lower leaves so as to ensure that one-third stem can be inserted in the soil. The leaves on the shoot will help in supplying food to the plant for root formation and growth. If the shoot bears flowers, remove them. Treat the cutting with 'rooting powder' which facilitates development of a healthy rooting system in the cutting. Insert one-third of the cutting in the soil medium. The cuttings are planted immediately to minimize shock effect and any loss. They are planted 1-2 inches apart in the coarse sand known to be the best medium for rooting. Place them in shade and keep misting with clean water to keep the leaf surface wet. It may take 10-15 days for Dahlia and Chrysanthemum while it may be 5-6 days for Marigold cuttings.

Semi-hard Wood Cutting: Only a few deciduous, evergreen shrubs and conifers are propagated by this method. All plants under this category propagate under the shade along with regular misting of water for maintaining high humidity around the cuttings. The propagation methodology is similar to soft wood cutting except that the size of the cuttings is increased to 14-22 cm. They are inserted half to one-third of the total length in the root medium after treatment with root-inducing hormones. It takes 4-6 weeks for the cutting to be ready for transplantation. Hibiscus, Hamelia and Jasmine are propagated by this method.

Hard Wood Cutting: Trees and shrubs are propagated by their mature shoots during their dormant phase (Jan-Feb in North India) when they are about to begin their growth. Rose, Bougainvillea and *Lagerstromia indica* are a few examples. The rooting medium for propagation of hard wood cutting is the same for soft and semi-hard wood cutting. Prepare 20-22 cm pencil-thick cuttings with a horizontal cut at its base and slanting cut at the top for maintaining the polarity while planting in the medium for rooting-thick cutting. Depending on the plant species hard wood cutting when treated with rooting hormone (IBA) 800-2000 ppm produce early and plentiful roots.

The cuttings are later inserted half the length at 45 degree angle in the sand at a distance of approximately 10 x 10 cm. Firm the soil from the sides and give regular misting to maintain the cuttings in moist condition. The rooting of cutting may take about 4-6 weeks depending on the environment. They are then transplanted in poly bags or earthen pots for further development.

Division

In this method multiplication is done by separating the clumps of Dahlia, suckers of Chrysanthemum, Gerbera, Asparagus and many other perennials. The

clumps are dug out from the ground and separated. Each separated plantlet is replanted in the ground or pots for further growth. This practice is followed during their dormant phase or during the rainy season when humidity is very high. Sometimes the overgrown clumps are thinned out by separating the offshoot. In this method, younger shoots are preferred to old central grown shoot for multiplication. Division is also done to reduce the excessive quantity of clumps and for weeding off the mature stock. Herbaceous perennial clumps are separated apart and the old and central ones are discarded and the outer portion bearing fresh growth is planted at a new site. Perennial Lupin and Delphinium are propagated by separating the cutting from the crown. Plants like Maranta and ferns are also multiplied by this method.

Seed Production

F-1 hybrid seeds of different flowers would perform best when grown once only. However, seeds collected from OP (open pollinated) varieties could be used in the following seasons. In a home garden, check on cross pollination is

difficult because of the presence of numerous varieties of flowers in beds. If, however, you wish to cultivate the seeds, then select the most promising plants for seed collection and bear the following points in mind:

▶ Regularly uproot the infected and unwanted flowering plants.

▶ As soon as the flowers appear, select a healthy flower with the required characteristics and use a tag for the purpose of identification.

▶ Paper bags can be tied around the plants to prevent dropping of seeds where the seed capsules burst or drop on maturity, e.g. Balsam, Pansy.

▶ Seeds are hand-picked manually from dry pods before the seeds are shed.

▶ The heads are generally thrashed by hand, winnowed and screened.

▶ The dry seeds are carefully stored in muslin bags and tagged with proper identification and kept in a dry and cool condition in a tight container.

▶ The seeds stored for the next year should be maintained at relative humidity below 20% and temperature around 10 degree C.

Post-Planting Care of Plants

Prosperous propagation of plants depends upon the success of all operations and is not confined to a single activity. The following garden activities are important and should be followed to ensure a good bloom.

Irrigation

To an amateur gardener, looking after garden means watering it plentifully: this is a myth. In other words, unwanted irrigation causes more damages to the plant than benefit. The quantum of water supplied to the plant depends upon the texture of the soil, size of the plant, growth phase, and climatic conditions. The water reqirement is more during the active growth phase and less during dormant growth phase. Small-sized plants need shallow irrigation while deep-rooted shrubs and trees require deep irrigation. Water requirement is more during the early phases of growth and flower formation. Accordingly, frequent irrigation is required during dry and hot weather and lesser during rainy and winter season. Maintenance of adequate moisture cannot be decided by fixing the frequency of irrigation but depends on the personal judgement considering the climatic condition. However, in general, plants require irrigation when the foliage shows signs of slight dropping. At this stage flooding can be done.

The appropriate time for irrigation is in the evening.

In the summers as the temperature soars up, watering in the evening prevents dehydration. It also helps fight the frost in the winter by creating a warmer medium around the plant. Avoid flooding the beds with a hosepipe when they are young as direct and strong stream of water can uproot the tender plants. Sprinkle water on the plants to give a rainy effect but do not sprinkle water on the flowers during the flowering period. Water penetration in the soil can be gauged by cutting the soil with a 'khurpi' in the bed. Moisture up to 14-22 cm is adequate. Avoid the soil to cake.

Light soils need lighter and more frequent irrigation in comparison to heavy soils. Poor quality of saline waters is not suitable for irrigation of these plants.

Weeding

Any unwanted plantation in a crop is a weed. Weeds grow with great vigour and pose a serious threat to the survival of the crop as they compete for space, sunlight and nutrients much needed by the plants. Therefore, weeds should be removed as soon as they are spotted.

Irrigate the bed prior to weeding so as to make the soil loose; never try weeding in dry and hard soil, as it will be difficult to remove the weed from its root. Weeding must be done at regular intervals prior to seed formation. Dispose the weeds into a pit dug separately in the corner of the house. When they are dry, burn them to ensure that they do not grow again. Some common weeds are motha (*Cyperus rotundus*) and oxalis, etc.

In a home garden chemical control should be avoided because of dense population of the seasonal flowers leaving no free space in between the weeds and the flowers. It is not commercially viable to spray expensive chemicals in small beds of home garden. Chemical control is more effective on broad-leaved weeds and during summer when the weeds are weak and dehydrated. While applying the spray ensure that the weather is calm (not windy) and any wanted plantation is not in immediate vicinity. Keep the nozzle of the spray pump vertically to the ground so that the spread does not move and damage the adjoining vegetation.

A very successful method to check the germination of weeds is spreading of a perforated synthetic sheet over the soil beds. As the sheet is porous it permits aeration of soil and ensures drainage and also discourages weed propagation.

Hoeing is done at optimum soil moisture conditions to improve air-water relation in root zone soil and to eliminate weeds. Expose the soil to the sun as the sunlight enriches the soil and kills harmful bacteria. Hoe the flower beds before irrigation.

Staking

Staking is done with a wooden or any other similar material, to support the plant to hold itself and later withstand the weight of the bloom. Top-heavy or weak-stemmed flowers of Dahlia, Chrysanthemum, etc. require staking. Trees and shrubs also require staking in the early years for establishment and to prevent lodging due to wind.

Staking is planned at the time of sowing of the flower, but it is done when the plant is about 14 cm in height or on 'as required' basis. Staking must be stable, firm and should not be erected too close to the roots of the plant to avoid damage. Thin bamboo cuttings of 2-4 cm diameter make an ideal staking material. Never use metallic material for staking as the metal's heat causes temperature shock to the plants. The staking should be replaced as the size of the plant

Staking

increases. In normal course, the single stake holds the plant with a cord tied to the stake and the plant. The length of the staking should be less than the height of the flower. However, to support a top-heavy flower, stakes are put all around the plant with tightly held cord. At times, the height of staking even rises above the flower top.

Pinching

Pinching is required to stop the growth on the main shoot and develops lateral shoots and, later, the shoots form sub-lateral shoots.

Pinching is done with the thumbnail and index finger to develop the plant into a bushy shape and also to prolong the flowering period. It is usually done after a month of transplanting and for 2-3 times to encourage bushy formation of plants. The best results are obtained when it is done early in the morning. Flowers like Carnation, Chrysanthemum, Cosmos, Nemesia, Petunia, Phlox, Marigold and Verbena are pinched in the early hours of the morning. Marigold is pinched during the vegetative phase to increase the number of branches and make it bushy. If not pinched, only single apical flowers will bloom. In case of the standard variety of Chrysanthemum, the apical bud is not pinched but the buds in axils of all leaves at four-week stage are removed as soon as they appear. On the other hand, to get a spray of flowers the apical bud is pinched to induce branching.

Disbudding

Disbudding and pinching are done for better spread and size of bloom in flowers. Removal of the buds from the stem of a flowering shoot is done to pave way for formation of large flowers. In spray types of small flower formation such as Chrysanthemum and Dahlia, pinching is done. In large varieties of Chrysanthemum and Dahlia, side-disbudding is done and central budding is done to allow its growth on all sides.

Picking of Spent Flower Buds

Picking is done when seeds are not required. Reproduction always takes priority, so, as soon as the flower withers pluck it. This activity transfers seed formation energy for a fresh spell of bloom.

Roguing

Uproot any off-type plants from beds as soon as these are recognized.

Points to Ponder:

* Take a walk around and inspect every part of the garden.

* Carry forward your observations to the gardener and check the work on the previous suggestions.

* While moving in the garden a cutter in hand is always handy for a gardener to prune any undesirable growth.

* Keep the garden neat and clean. Remove dead branches from all the plantations.

* Spray the foliage plant to remove dust and maintain a much required moist atmosphere.

* A green layer of algae on the top layer of the soil is a sign of a moist and shady place.

* Vigilantly observe the plants for a possible incest or disease attack. Accordingly, examine the soil periodically.

* Ensure that shade-loving plants are kept under proper shade. Plants requiring protection from frost must be covered well.

* Maintain an inventory of basic garden implements and keep them clean and operational. Keep handy a 'khurpi' for weeding and hoeing. A dibbler and trowel should be kept for planting and transplanting of plants, pruning knife and pruning shears for pruning and trimming. Watering is done using hosepipe fitted with nozzle or by a water-can. A hand-spray pump must be kept available for spraying insecticides and pesticides.

* Regularly service your lawn-mower for its smooth running and sharpened blades. After every cutting, wash the lawn-mower and oil the blades with drops of used mobile oil to prevent rusting of the blades.

* A diary always proves handy to remember previously jotted and fresh points.

Manures and Fertilizers for Garden Flowers

Good soil health is the pre-requisite for successful cultivation of any crop plant. The primary nutrients for the growth and development of the plants are Nitrogen (N), Phosphorous (P), and Potassium (K). Continuous cultivation, growth of weeds, leaching, erosion and volatilization render the soil deficient in these nutrients. The deficiency of these nutrients in the soil can be ameliorated by application of manures and fertilizers. Manures have a slow and lasting impact while chemical fertilizers have immediate and short-lived effect on the plant. Manures are less washable than chemical fertilizers; however, a balanced application of both manures and fertilizers yields best results.

Manures

Aeration and enriching soil with macro and micro nutrients helps in retaining more moisture in the growing media. Manures are derived from residues of plants and animals and add organic matter in the soil. Organic matter in the soil has three major functions. First, it acts as a reservoir for nutrients. Secondly, it provides humus-forming material which improves the moisture holding capacity of the soil. Thirdly, it makes the soil alive by increasing activity of micro-organisms. These micro-organisms mineralize organic form of minerals/ nutrients into simpler forms, which can be absorbed by the plants. The advantage of organic manure is that they are safe as any overdose gets catered for and they disintegrate slowly, thereby making the nutrients available for a longer period of time. The commonly used manures are:

1. Farmyard Manure (FYM)

It is a complete manure and by and large meets all the requirements of the plant. A well-composed FYM has the following nutrients:

Nitrogen	-	0.5%
Phosphorus	-	0.2%
Potash	-	0.5%

It consists of dung, urine and refuse of cattle-shed which is collected on daily basis in a pit approximately 6 m long, 2 m wide and 1 m deep. The pit is filled 1-2 feet above the ground and plastered with the slurry of the dung and soil which is left undisturbed for four to six months for the anaerobic micro-organism to undertake fermentation.

FYM is matured either in heaps or pits. The harmful pathogenic organisms are killed due to high temperature in heaps and toxins in pits during decomposition. The freely available air in a heap hastens the rate of decomposition and also raises the temperature which causes loss of organic material reducing it to 50 per cent. The moisture content is also reduced, especially during peak summer and it decreases the rate of decomposition. There is substantial loss of nutrients during the rainy season in the heap outdoors. Pits do not have the above limitations but have the advantage of conserving organic matter with a loss of only 20 per cent.

Never use undecomposed dung for farmyard manure as it immobilizes the nutrients. On an average, farmyard manure must be applied twice a year, once prior to winter cultivation and other before the summer cultivation of seasonal flowers. Avoid heaping the FYM for longer duration in the beds, as nutrients are lost when exposed to the sun. It should be immediately spread over the soil and mixed thoroughly. In urban areas the storage of FYM poses a problem. Dry the FYM and store it in a polythene bag or container and seal it properly. You may lose some percentage of nutrients due to absence of moisture but it will prevent spread of bad odour in the house.

The poultry manure is richer than farmyard manure but if used half compost, it emits foul smell for a while. Poultry manure should be mixed with farmyard manure into the pit, and covered with a layer of soil and allowed to age.

2. Compost

It is a technique to utilize the organic waste into productive usage. The garden waste, kitchen refuse, household garbage and wood shavings when put into the garbage bin, form excellent ingredients of compost. All these materials being organic in nature get decomposed with the help of bacteria when subjected to anaerobic

decomposition and form manure rich in nutrients. It contains Nitrogen (0.5%), Phosphorus (0.15%), and Potassium (0.5%).

Dig a pit in a suitable well-drained location in the garden about 5 m long, 2 m wide and 1 m deep in an area having partial shade as sunlight during summer kills the bacteria to a large extent. Sprinkle limestone in the empty pit and heap up the pit with layers of different organic materials and soil to form a concave top to retain water. Turn the pile regularly and moisten the layers. It takes three to four months to turn it into complete compost. Prepare several compost pits with a few weeks' gap for round-the-year supply. Do not dispose off material like polythene bags, etc. in the pit as these will never disintegrate into organic manure. Compost is a good source of nutrients.

In general, the garden and home waste is dumped to form compost while few gardeners have them separately. To get leaf mould, garden waste, garden sweepings, dry foliage and dry woody material is decomposed along with a small proportion of soil. In normal conditions, it takes 9-12 months for the leaves to be reduced to convert into mould, while the period gets shortened under moist conditions. It also increases the humus in the soil; therefore, can be applied to sandy and clayey soils. Its application, at least once a year, is beneficial. Leaf mould brings down the 'ph-level' of the soil and is best suitable for acidic soils.

3. Liquid Manure

Cow-dung in excess of water forms liquid manure. It is the most effective manure as the nutrients are made available to the plant in the immediately useable form and the results are obtained in a very short time.

Take a given quantity of fresh cow-dung and put it in a container filled with three times the quantity of water. Alternatively, mix cow-dung and powdered oil cakes of 'karai' or mustard or 'mahow' cakes. Allow the fermentation to take place that shall depend upon the weather condition. Add 25-30 times water in it to make it a clear solution of light tea colour which as a thumb rule is considered safe for application. Take a mug and spill it over the moist soil bed of a well-established actively growing plantation. As a caution do not spill over the foliage of the plant. It is most effective to the flowers during bud formation stage. Fertilizers are also applied in liquid form in the given dilution: In 100 litre of water, add 60 gram of CAN or 45 gram of DAP or 45 gram of urea.

4. Concentrated Organic Manures

These are the by-products of the plants and animals which are organic in nature and possess high percentage of NPK. These are readily available in the market and need not be prepared in the home garden. The cost of these is relatively on the higher side in comparison to that of chemical fertilizers. These should be supplemented with chemical fertilizers as and when required depending upon the deficiency in soil and need of the plant.

Oil cakes are residues of the seeds of castor, groundnut, rapeseed and mustard after oil extraction from them, which are rich in nitrogen (3-5%), phosphorus (1-2%) and proteins. They also contain a small percentage of potash and phosphorus. The oil cake lumps are broken and powdered for easy broadcast and decomposition. Oil cakes can also be applied to the moist soil while preparing the beds and used later as top dressing on the soil.

Fish meal holds a large percentage of nitrogen (4-10%) and phosphorus (3-9%) and is considered as well-balanced organic manure. Bone meal contains high amount of calcium (20-25%), phosphorus and nitrogen. It is suitable for acidic soil and used for growing flowers in pots. Blood meal is rich in nitrogen content (12-15%). Wood ash is high in potash.

Fertilizers

These are industrially manufactured chemical fertilizers and are important to the plants because these provide concentrated doses of nutrients and trace elements, which are not present in required quantity in the soil. Since these are in concentrated form they should be used very cautiously. As a thumb rule, little less is better than little more. This is because a high concentration of chemical would cause the plant to lose water by the process of ex-osmosis from their roots. They are acidic/alkaline in reaction and overdose or regular use for longer period will have harmful effects on plants. These fertilizers are used for specific deficiency and at a specific time. Essentially, use inorganic fertilizers as supplement rather than as substitute to organic manure.

Important Fertilizers

There are mainly three types of commonly used fertilizers.

1. Nitrogenous Fertilizers

These are readily absorbed by the plants and results are seen within few days of application. Do not apply to a dry soil; the soil must be moist and a light application of water is advisable thereafter. They are

highly soluble and therefore should be applied in small quantities to avoid leaching. A direct contact with the foliage must be avoided. Some common nitrogenous fertilizers are Ammonium Sulphate (20%), Calcium Ammonium Nitrate (CAN) (25%), and Urea (46%).

Fertilizers like urea or ammonia or sulphate in the ratio of 2 gram/litre or 30 gram can be dissolved in 15 litres of water for effective results. As top dressing, urea is most widely used as it contains a high percentage of nitrogen.

2. Phosphate Fertilizers

Commonly used phosphate fertilizers are Single Superphosphate (16%) and Di-ammonium Phosphate (46%). Requirement of phosphate is high during the early growth phase. Phosphates are least mobile. Therefore, they must be made available close to the roots. They are, thus, mixed in the soil during sowing.

3. Potassic Fertilizers

Potassium chloride, commonly known as muriate of potash (60%), is suitable to all plants and is generally applied before sowing. Potash is required during the early phase and it builds resistance towards diseases. Prefer use of potassium sulphate in soils with high pH value.

Complex fertilizers provide two or more than two nutrients. The commonly used complex fertilizers are:

▶ Di-Ammonium Phosphate (DAP) – 18% N and 48% P;

▶ NPK in various combinations, the most common being 12-32-16 containing 12% N, 32% P and 16% K, respectively.

Other Nutrients

Some nutrients, viz., calcium, magnesium, sulphur, iron, copper, chlorine, boron, Mn, Mo and zinc are essential for plant growth and are required in very small quantity. However, their deficiency leads to yellowing of leaves, reduced growth and flower formation. Nutrients like iron, zinc, manganese, magnesium and copper may be sprayed on the plants if adequate organic manure is not applied. Multi-micronutrients are also available in the market. The recommended dose is 3 gram in one litre of water and at least two sprays (or depending upon the extent of deficiency) are required during the peak growth phase, i.e., 3-4 weeks after transplantation and 2-3 weeks after the first spray.

Application Methodology

As a general rule, nitrogenous fertilizers have split application while phosphorous and potassium is mixed in the soil at the time of preparing the soil beds.

Points to Ponder:

* The soil should be tested for its suitability before administrating any inorganic fertilizer.
* Use the suggested fertilizer at the prescribed time in the recommended dosage.
* Organic manure should be thoroughly mixed with soil.
* Use one inorganic fertilizer at a time so as to avoid any reaction unless advised by an expert.
* Watering is must after application of inorganic fertilizers.
* Avoid direct contact of fertilizers with foliage.
* Do not throw weeds in the manure pit as their seeds will find way into the soil bed when manure is applied.

Growing Flowers in Pots

Importance of Pot Flower

The essence of pot gardening lies in its mobility. The pots constitute an essential component of a garden and create an outstanding aura. A garden without pot plants is incomplete and gives a blank look. They are used as fillers and cover-up plants to hide bad patches by placing the pots on them and rendering colour to dull places. The climbers grown in pots are spread on the unsightly looking and unfinished walls in and around the garden. Pots increase the ground coverage area by extending the garden to inaccessible areas both indoors and outdoors, viz., along the stairs, pavements, in rooms, verandahs, on projections and rooftops. The mobility gives the option to carry them off to any part of the house and gives the flexibility to change arrangement to form new and fresh patterns. In window gardens, place the pots at the windows facing east, west or south so that the plant can have at least 4-6 hours of sunlight. Use the eastern side window or the window in interior with semi-diffused light for shade-loving plants like Cineraria and Salvia.

It is interesting to note that indoor plants are more dependent on the gardener than outdoor plants or the care indoor plants require is much more than outdoor ones.

Choice of Plants

Right selection is crucial for the survival and growth of the plant as a few plants thrive better in pots while others do not. Seasonal flowers, which are generally grown in pots, are Aster, Brachycome, Cineraria, Chrysanthemum, Dahlia (raised from cuttings), Nemesia, Pansy, Petunia and Portluca, etc. The beauty of flower pots is short-lived depending upon the flowering span. However, foliage plants provide greenery throughout the year.

Choice of Pot

The pots are available in various shapes and sizes for example round, square, hexagonal, etc. and range in size from 3 inches to 15 inches in diameter with a depth of 2 inches to 18 inches. Bigger pots are also available but they are too bulky to be carried from one place to another and lose the advantage of mobility. The pot size is chosen considering the growth potential of the plant as it should be neither too small nor too big in relation to the plant so as to give an odd look. A pot will always display a better look if the foliage covers the entire pot.

The next consideration is the texture of pot material. While choosing a pot never get fascinated by the looks and have the impression that a costly pot is a fine material. The need of the plant cannot be ignored and you should know that plants thrive better in clay earthenware as the roots can breathe and absorb moisture. Other alternatives are pots made of brazen, wooden and synthetic material but ensure these pots should retain their external finish and are of lasting nature. A metallic pot has the major disadvantage of causing temperature shock to the plant due to rise and fall of temperature during the day and night, respectively. The metals produce harmful bi-products with the reaction of chemical in the soil. Avoid painting earthen or cemented pots to make them look elegant as this will inhibit aeration of the porous material. Also keep in mind that a decorative and colourful pot will always outshine the plant in it.

Pots placed in a jardiniere bigger in size are also in use. The drained water collected at the base needs to be removed regularly. A drain plate at the base of the pot helps collect the excess water that gets spilled from the pot. This also does not cause forming of a permanent mark of the spill on the floor.

Whatever may be the size, shape or texture, the most important thing is that it should have an appropriate drainage hole at the base to let excess water pour out.

Always use a pot with a drainage hole at the bottom.

Preparation of Pot Soil

A general purpose mixture is prepared by mixing the following ingredients in the ratio of 2:1:1/2:1/2.

- Two parts of garden soil;
- One part leaf-mould;
- Half part sand; and
- Half part farmyard manure.

Add super phosphate (1 kg), ammonium sulphate (1/2 kg) and muriates of potash (2/4 kg) per cubic meter of the soil mix. Treat the soil with anti-termite Cholorpyrphos 20EC by dissolving 2 ml of the solution in one litre of water and pouring it in the pot till water drops start dripping out from the drainage hole. The lumps are broken and the soil is then turned number of times to form a fine texture. In case the pot mixture is dry, spray a light shower of water to make it moist and to facilitate setting of the soil.

New pots are prepared by soaking them in water for a few minutes and then allowed to dry. This is done to reduce moisture absorption from the soil mixture. First, ensure that the drainage hole is open, clear and of good-size. Secondly, take a large piece of crock and cover the hole with the concave side on the hole to ensure that it does not get blocked. Now place a few more small pieces of crocks or gravel to form a thick layer. Thirdly, spread a thin layer of leaf mould to prevent the soil mixture from seeping to block the drainage hole. Next, fill the pot with the soil mixture in layers and gently press each layer so that the soil gets well settled but does not become hard. Fix the seedlings keeping in mind that the spread should cover the pot completely. While planting permanent plants remove

soil equivalent to the size of the root ball and transfer the same in the dug-out place in the pot. Now gently start pouring the soil mixture and press each layer to ensure that the plant fixes in properly and there is no pressure on the roots in this process so as to get damaged. The soil mixture should be lower by 2-1 inches from the top of the rim to accommodate water. The watering of the pot should be done with a low-pressure shower.

Care of Pots

When we think of care of potted plants, air, water, sunlight and temperature are the essential components which should be catered to adequately.

AIR is essential for the healthy growth of all living beings. Therefore, all plants need good ventilation.

WATER is essential to all plants but what is equally important is when to water and how much to water.

A porous pot has the advantage of good aeration but it dries faster than glazed pots. Pots placed at a warmer location need more water than those placed at a lower temperature. If the quantum of sunlight falling on the plant is high, more water intake is required. Water intake increases during active stages of growth rather than in dormant phases. The water requirement varies from plant to plant, as few need more than others do. An easy way to judge whether the pot needs watering is to tap the pot with knuckles. An empty or hollow sound indicates that watering is needed.

Water is never sprinkled on top of the foliage but at the base of the plant with a low-pressure hose till the water just starts dripping from the drainage hole. Watering can also be done by submerging the pot to two-third its height in a container filled with water where the water enters the pot from the bottom through the drainage hole. Do not over-water the pots as this drains away the nutrients. Regularly remove excess water in the jardiniere. Tilt the pots to drain excessive rainwater during the rainy season.

SUNLIGHT even for a part of the day is essential for flowering though indirect light is enough for the growth of foliage. It is important to take a note of the sunshine requirement while selecting indoor plants. Pot plants kept indoors or under shade tend to bend towards the direction of sunlight. To check this lop-sided growth, the location of the pots may be either changed or rotated periodically or pots are shifted outdoors for a couple of days in a shady place rather than under direct sun to avoid temperature shock.

A sudden change of temperature is harmful for the plants; therefore, such differences should be avoided. Be careful while using metallic pots as these often cause such variations.

It should be kept in mind that our homes are warmer than outdoors and a warmer place will have low humidity level.

MANURE once a week in the form of liquid manure should be preferred to fertilizers. Manuring is done during the growth phase rather than dormant phase.

If you happen to go out on vacation, bury the flowering pots in the soil up to the rim in a partial shady place in your house and water them. This exercise considerably reduces water requirement. A piece of stone below the pothole prevents worms from getting inside the pot.

The main reasons for failure of pot plants are that we fail to understand the requirement of the flowering plant we select. Secondly, we must know that these requirements can be met in our garden.

Preparing Pot Flowers for Flower Show – Few Essential Tips

Where and when: The sowing of the seed should be done in the reverse calculation from the day the flower show is to be held. Thus, keeping track of the time-schedule is utmost important.

The organizers: It does not contribute as who is organizing the flower show but it helps you to understand the mind-set of the organizer.

Rules and regulations: Study the instructions taking a previous year copy or advance copy to avoid disqualification or losing points thereafter. Be particular about the specifications, number of entries, groups in which pots are presented, timings, etc.

Categories of contest: Be sure of the category to be contested and label them in clear showing their class and section.

Cut flowers in flower show: Ensure to carry the quantum of the required material in the size and length (of the stem) as indicated in the rules.

Selection of contest material: A detailed study and expert help in this regard is beneficial.

Presentation technique: Make notes from the previous flower shows attended and take guidance from regular participants so that the material is the best one used.

Point scoring system: Participants must educate themselves with the scoring system to draw maximum points in the competition.

Important Guidelines

- The flowers should be sown considering the date in reverse calculation so as to have the best bloom at that time.
- It is advisable to sow the plants with a gap of 4-5 days to cater for any failure in the crop and present the best bloom in the show.
- Selection of the size of pot in relation to the plant sown can make a big difference in the effect it gives. Only one plant is sown per pot and if the plant is not in proportion with the pot it will give a hollow effect.
- Post-care operations, i.e., irrigation, hoeing, staking, disbudding and pinching, etc. are very important to yield the best bloom. Manure and fertilization application directly affect the bloom.
- Remember, disbudding is done to take large flowers on the apical bud while pinching makes the plant bushy.
- Freshly transplanted plants should be summarily rejected and not considered for the competition.
- The leaves of the plants should be cleaned giving a light spray of water with a hand-spray. The pots should be cleaned with sand paper and painted with terracotta red.
- Staking of stems, covering of plant to avoid being bruised, catering for extra pots are a few transit risks that should be taken care of.
- Concealed identification making should be done for the pots in order to prevent likely mixing or theft.
- A rehearsal prior to participation for displaying technique will give added advantage.

Points to Ponder:

- Place plants in appropriate pots with pot to flower ratio as 3:5.
- Use burnt clay pots instead of non-porous and showy pots.
- Prepare the soil mixture according to the requirements of the plant.
- Potting and re-potting should be done as per the method described.
- Never grow tall and profusely branched plants in pots.
- Plants with heavy and compact bloom are most suitable for pots.
- Pot plants require more time and care than ground plants.

Garden Flowers in Floral Arrangement

Flower arrangement brings a touch of natural beauty and transpires the effect of garden indoors. Flowers sneak into every room in a house and find a central place in formal places as well as at functions. If making a flower arrangement is your passion, grow flowers and foliage which are extensively used as cut flowers in flower arrangements. The details regarding choosing the flowers which are used as cut flowers are given in the text facing the respective flower plate. This will make available the fresh flowers at your doorstep at a much less cost and also reduce your dependency for purchasing them from the open market. Gerbera, Gladiolus, Carnation, and Cornflower are few flowers which are used as cut flowers and find place in flower arrangements. This chapter contains just the basic theory; however, flower arrangement is a practical art which is perfected by experience.

It is an art of preserving the nature's splendour and arranging the same with creativity, in spectrum of designs according to the occasion and to match the location of the room. The permutation of colours, choice of flowers and diversity in arrangement is beyond imagination. A nicely arranged and well-prepared flower arrangement adds beauty and charm and makes the place lively. The arrangement may be short-lived but the pleasure and delight is immense.

However, practice and experience develops more understanding and subsequently sharpens your skills. In the absence of fresh and dry flowers, flower arrangement can also be made using artificial flowers and foliage along with other material. These days there is increasing trend of using flowers in day-to-day life as it fits even in a small budget.

Principles of Flower Arrangement

There are a few basic principles which should be observed as general guidelines for making arrangements and by following these one can be sure of producing a pleasing and harmonious composition. These principles are universal to any style of flower arrangement which is as below:

❱ Proportion is the ratio which is soothing and pleasing to the eye. Greeks had developed proportions based on their study and experience and suggested that ratios of 2:3 and 3:5 in case of flat arrangements (two-dimensional), and 5:7:11 in case of solid arrangements (three-dimensional) give good visual effect.

❱ Balance helps to create a feeling of rest and repose by arranging or grouping flowers, foliage and colours around a central point to make an equalization of material on each side of the central point of the arrangement. It can be achieved both formally and informally. A formal (symmetrical) balance results

when identical material of equal attraction are placed at equidistance from the central point while informal (asymmetrical) balance is caused when material of unequal attraction are placed at different distance away from the central point. An informal arrangement is more interesting.

▸ A stable and self-supporting arrangement maintains a proper balance by placing large and deepest flowers in the centre of asymmetrical or symmetrical balance. To have the best effect, the arrangement must be made in good proportion having proper sizes, with the most vibrant and showy flowers in the centre and the smallest towards the periphery. Large flower arrangements with varying size of flowers create an impressive design. If the arrangements are to be made identical then symmetry is to be kept in mind.

▸ Emphasis is developed by creating a focal point or centre of interest or accent in the geometric centre above the lip of the container. Large, open and bright coloured flowers against a dark background also create an interesting look. The background of the place should be less conspicuous than the arrangement. Plain walls and curtains make an ideal background. However, it is important to keep in mind:

What to emphasize, how to emphasize, where to emphasize, and how much to emphasize.

▸ Depth in the arrangement is necessary otherwise it will give a flat appearance. It should not look like a stuffed material but form pattern in continuity of the material used with harmony of colours.

▸ Rhythm is created in the design with gradation of the coloured flowers and metarials in such a way that the eyeball moves from one corner to the other with ease, in a connected path, in a related movement without losing interest of the focal point. The movement can be created by repetition of shapes and progression of sizes in an arrangement.

▸ Harmony produces the impression of unity through the selection and arrangement of consistent materials. All the likeness among the materials used creates a feeling of unity while too much of mandatory development by repetition should be corrected by using contrasts. Harmony is created when all the components fit and blend together to project a single idea. It is achieved by using materials and flowers which blend easily rather than using flowers of different types and colours. The element of contrast, light and dark and smooth against rough, cannot be ignored. Light and fine material is to be placed at the top so as to allow light to pass, while dark and dense material towards the base to absorb the light.

Styles of Flower Arrangement

There are two basic styles of flower arrangements. European or Western Style is a style with liberal school of thought and is based on mass effect. It is formed by large, closely-packed flowers with varied colours. The shapes could be round, oval, triangular, L-shaped, S-shaped and crescent-shaped. To start with, an outline of the exact shape of the arrangement is drawn. It is followed by embedding flowers as 'points' and is made compact with 'fillers'. Focus is stretched from the individual flower to a mass effect. The overall effect is like growing a plant in a natural form causing a radiant effect, heavier at base and flowing outward.

Oriental or Eastern or Ikebana Style originated in China and was later developed by the Japanese. It is based on religious and philosophical principles. This is the simplest style of flower arrangement and is designed for religious purposes, the emphasis being more on the theme and individual material than on the mass effect. Heaven, Man and Earth are the guiding principles of all arrangements. A typical design has three components. A fully open, half open and tight bud denotes past, present and future, respectively. The emphasis is mainly on three lines, the tallest branch known as 'shin' is one-and-a-half to two times the length of the vase. The second line, 'soe' is three-fourth the length of the shin. The third 'hikae' is three-fourth the length of 'soe'. Under no circumstances the material touches the rim of the vase. By nature, the side branches lean towards side, back and upwards. In fact, the flowers should always look upwards. These arrangements are to be viewed from the front side and thus are asymmetrical in nature.

The Western and Eastern styles fuse to form another style known as 'geometric design' which is a line-mass combine. There are few differences in both the styles; in Western Style, the flower looks upwards or downwards while in Eastern it always looks upwards. There is no use of wire net in the Eastern Style and the shells, bark, and dry branches are used to emulate nature. The material may be of any type but these must go well with the flower material and should blend with the arrangement.

Choosing Containers/Vases

A right selection of vase, flowers and other materials add charm to the room. The vase must match the colour of flowers and room or vice versa. Shades of yellow, brown, green and white generally go well with flower hues. A statue beside the base or adding stones at the base can lend an interesting look to the vase. Low and Western table arrangements look attractive with round and oval bowls. Fan-shaped and triangular styles look well in vases with stem, which causes the material to flow out and droop down.

Preparing the Container

▶ Wash the container thoroughly.

▶ While using wire netting for making Western arrangements, ensure it does not come out from the container.

▶ In tall arrangements put few pebbles in the vase to make the base heavy and to avoid toppling.

▶ Similarly, firm the pin holder if you know the distribution of foliage is uneven and can cause tilt of the vase.

Collection of Flowers

It is prime most to know the flowers which are used in flower arrangements. Secondly, it is equally important to know at which stage the flower is to be cut for the arrangement. The flowers are graded according to their size, colour, freshness and length of the stem. Select the best flowering shoot with a long stem, full in vigour and free from diseases. Flowers are generally cut in the bud stage early in the morning or in the evening as they always last longer. Use a pair of scissors or a garden cutter and chop off the stem from a plentiful location and avoid tearing off the stem. In case the flower is to be carried to a distant location, gently shake off the water drops and place the flower in a polythene bag with the flower head first. Blow air to fill the bag and secure

A Symmetrical Flower Arrangement

An Asymmetrical Flower Arrangement

Tools and Equipments Required

* Large and small buckets with double handle
* Florist scissors with serrated blades
* A pair of pliers for cutting wires (never use scissors)
* Floral foam, pin holder and wire netting
* Florist's wire for supporting the stems
* Wire mesh to strengthen foam
* Floral tape
* Misters for spraying
* Knife
* Bases
* Vases
* Accessories – decorative items, e.g. candles, figures, shells
* Old newspapers

the open end using a rubber band or a thread. The flower heads must be pointing downwards while they are carried away from the garden.

Once back at home, withdraw the stems from the polythene and trim the stems according to the need. The cut given to the stem should not be horizontal as the shoot will settle flat on the bottom and retard intake of water. A slant cut increases the surface area causing rapid absorption of water. Insert the hollow stem into the water quickly otherwise the sap will ooze and block the intake of water in the stem (for example, Dahlias, Poppies, etc).

Preparing the Stem

A majority of flowers and foliage can be conditioned in a common way but some need extra care. Give a deep drink of water for a minimum of two to three hours. However, an overnight dip should be preferred. Thereafter, to prolong flowering duration, plunge the flower up to the flower head in a vessel filled with lukewarm water. Soft leaves are submerged in a pan containing water. If the stem is soft and not rigid, wrap it in non-greasy paper so that the stem remains straight during the process of deep drink. If the stems are woody, they should be immersed up to 2-3 cm in boiling hot water. Make a hole in the cardboard or hard sheet to protect the petals from the heat of the water vapours. Otherwise wrap a cloth or paper around the flower and then place the shoot in the boiling water. Hard stems of Carnation are given a deep cut at the centre of the stem up to one-third of their length. In case of Chrysanthemum, the stem is hammered at the bottom to enable more water intake by the flower.

The cut flowers are then kept in a shady, moist and cool place away from direct sunlight and heat. Ideally an air-conditioned room provides optimum storage conditions. Never carry or store the cut flowers in a windy area. Wilting flowers can be revived by knocking off 2-3 cm of the stem under water and dipping it in water.

Selection of Foliage

The foliage must blend and harmonize with the floral design and should have matching lifespan and vigour with the flowers. The foliage of common permanent plants can be used in arrangements as these can withstand indoor conditions. What is meaningful is to know the texture of the leaf instead of the stem. The criteria for choosing the foliage are same as for the flowers except in flowers we take young buds but in foliage, middle-aged foliage should be taken. Damaged, mature and wilted foliage should never be taken. In unavoidable conditions trim the damaged edges with scissors. After selection of the foliage wash it well and keep

Material for flower arrangement as displayed in a shop.

SHAPE OF VASE	STYLE OF FLORAL DESIGN
Very small containers	Miniature arrangements
Flat-shaped	Tall-medium-low arrangements
Bowl-shaped	Tall-medium-low arrangements
Vase with short stem	Medium arrangements
Vase with long stem	Tall arrangements
Basket-flat	Tall-medium-low arrangements
Basket-bowl	Tall-medium-low arrangements

it in a cool place. Minimize the use of pins and stapler pins to hold the foliage as it damages the foliage and casts an ugly look rather than a pleasing effect to the arrangement.

Factors Influencing the Floral Design

In general, a few factors are to be kept in mind before making a flower arrangement. The prime most is the location/place where the arrangement is to be kept (i.e., on a dinning table or a sideboard). The location must be such that it should automatically draw attention at the first place. The availability of space is a determining factor as the size of the arrangement will vary accordingly. The height/level at which the arrangement is to be kept is the next factor. Finally, the viewing angle – if it is to be seen from one side or from all the sides. To get an all-sided view, shapes like oval, round and pyramid are preferred. There are no fixed standards but the more closer you are in arranging the flowers and other materials in a natural way, the more appealing the arrangement will look.

Types of Arrangements

Fresh Arrangement: It is the art of organizing fresh flowers and other plant material into vases and giving them a pleasing composition.

Foliage Arrangement: In seasons when flowers are scarce, variety of coloured leaves may be used to make these arrangements which harmonize well. These provide beautiful transitional lines and unify the base.

Dry Arrangement: These are composed of dried flowers, fruits, berries, stalks, pods, cones and drift wood which collectively produce a wonderful effect. These can be used as a substitute for fresh flowers and are somewhat permanent arrangement.

Fresh-cum-Dry Arrangement: These floral designs may be made by combining fresh and dry plant material for creating beautiful textural effects and variations.

Miniature or Diminutive Arrangement: To add aesthetic value to the study table, bathrooms and dressing table, floral compositions are created which are the miniature forms of the standard sizes.

Useful Tips:

▶ A flower arrangement is prepared to last for 4-6 days.

▶ Always cut longer stems at the site and bring them to the desired size while making the arrangement.

▶ To maintain regular flow of water insert the thin stem into the thicker stem and then fix it in the arrangement.

▶ Geometric designs are made by fixing the material at angles on the holder.

▶ If a material is to be pulled from the arrangement do it gently by pressing the holder and pulling the material from the middle without disturbing the arrangement.

▶ Drooping flowers are a symptom of scarcity of water which is met by cutting 2-3 cm of the stem and dipping it in warm water for two hours.

▶ There are six colour schemes and one can take help of a colour wheel while choosing colours.

▶ Related or contrasting colour harmonies may be followed for selection of colour.

Steps for Making Flower Arrangements

There are some common steps for making flower arrangements. However, variation may be accorded while creating a composition.

▶ Plan the framework in your mind considering the purpose, location, height and the space available. Generally 5-7 stems are sufficient to form the outline.

▶ Select containers/vases, flowers and foliage that express the mood of the occasion and room.

▶ The flowers should be according to the size and shape of the vase. Cut the stems into short, medium and tall lengths.

▶ The outline stems should be natural and not scattered in an arbitrary fashion.

▶ Arrange the tallest (with a supporting stick, if required) and the broad material first. Then place the remaining stems according to the type of the arrangement. Have one leading line and others supporting it.

▶ Create the 'focal point' low and near the centre. Large flowers with bright colours can be used in small numbers at the centre as they will add attraction due to their bigger size, distinctive shape and vibrant colours (e.g., Anthurium, Carnation and Gerbera). In tall vases, small flowers may be arranged in groups. The complete arrangement should maintain proportion between size and shape of the vase and plant material used.

▶ Slender/light stems and buds can be placed near the top of the arrangement.

▶ The 'line flowers' form the framework of the

design. These consist of flowers with thin, erect stems which provide a sense of height to the arrangement. Gladiolus, Delphinium, Snapdragons and Stocks are some common 'line flowers'.

▶ The fillers/foliage help to cover gaps, create contrast in the texture and add depth to the arrangement. Flowers of Gypsophilla, Statice, Lady's Lace, foliage like ferns, asparagus, money plants, etc. and buds of roses form excellent fillers.

▶ Cover the lower base of the container/vase with sufficient foliage.

▶ Pour enough water.

▶ Never oil the leaves but spray highlighter on the foliage if required. Use glittering sparkles to embellish the flowers.

▶ Finally, view the arrangement from a distance to spot loopholes.

Post Care of Arrangements

▶ Place the arrangement away from a windy place, drought conditions, source of heat (electricity lamp, top of television, etc.) and direct sunlight.

▶ If possible shift the arrangement to a cooler place at night or, alternately, cover it with a thin muslin wet cloth at night.

▶ A spray of water in the morning and evening will prolong the life of the arrangement and give it a fresh look.

▶ In general, the water is topped up daily but in case of flowers which last longer water should be changed frequently followed by cutting the stem to about 2-3 cm.

Useful Tips:

▶ Administer warm water for initial drink.

▶ Do not leave the cut flower out of water for a long period.

▶ Most elegant arrangements can be created using the humblest materials.

▶ Select a container according to the occasion and type of the flower arrangement.

Colour dyes are also used to enhance the colour of flowers.

▶ Sunlight hastens bacterial activity and produces foul odour. Therefore, it is advisable to wash the vase with water and sterilize it with a weak solution of bleaching powder. Put pieces of charcoal in the vase and top it with water.

▶ Regular change of water, wetting of flower and covering them with wet muslin cloth during night will make them last longer.

SHAPES OF ARRANGEMENTS

Types	Shape	Suitable Place
Line Arrangement a) Vertical arrangement: stems from the central point move upwards about twice the height of the container. b) Horizontal arrangement: stems radiate in all directions from the focal point in the centre.		a) Sideboard, tables b) Window sill, tables
Triangle a) Equilateral triangle: a traditional design in which all three sides of the floral design are of equal length which gives a one-sided view (symmetrical-formal). b) Isosceles triangle: the two sides are equal in length having the base or the third side of unequal length. It gives a one-sided view (symmetrical-informal). c) Right-angled triangle/L-shaped: an arrangement in which the vertical line is perpendicular to the base line (symmetrical-informal). d) Scalene triangle: it has unequal sides and angles. The floral arrangement has a vertical emphasis by extending the base line downwards (symmetrical-informal).		Side tables, corners, side shelve on walls, entrance, reception area

SHAPES OF ARRANGEMENTS

Types	Shape	Suitable Place
Round-Bowl These are medium height arrangements in round shape.	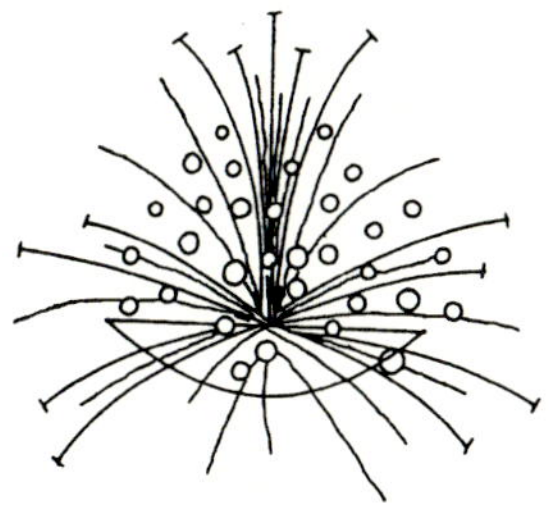	Side shelves, study table, window sill
Oval-Shaped These are low/flat, all-round balanced arrangements which can be viewed from all sides.	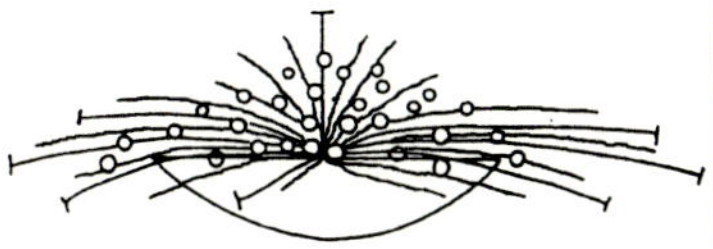	Centre table, dining table, conference table
Crescent/Moon-Shaped These are arrangements forming into a crescent shape of the moon.	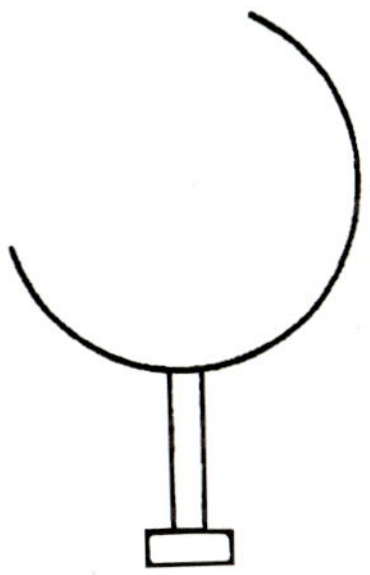	Side shelves, study tables, window sill
S-Shaped These are tall arrangements in 'S' shape.	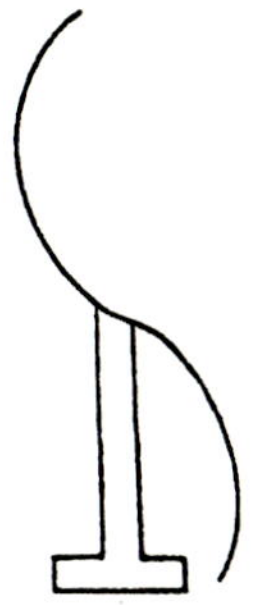	Side tables, corners

Dried Flowers

The desire to enjoy the exquisite beauty of seasonal flowers during off-season and non-availability of fresh flowers and foliage round the year has raised the demand for dried flowers. The aesthetic value, novelty, longevity and flexibility have made them unique and different. Dried flowers can also be carried away from their natural habitat making people enjoy their beauty in far-off places.

The drying of flowers though expensive is worth the money and time one spends as they offer the same beauty as fresh flowers, give near-natural looks, entail no maintenance cost, are eco-friendly, bio-degradable, have a long life and possess lasting value. Dried flowers find place indoors both in formal and informal places. They make floral craft items, wall hangings, floral balls, bouquets, collages, flower pictures, festival decorations and small items like greeting cards, calendars, and floral albums for flower identification. Further integration of dry fruits, dry roots, seashells, etc. lends a wide range to creativity while making various arrangements. The average life of a dried flower varies from six to twelve months; thereafter, they lose their elegance.

Selection of Material

Choose a perfect specimen making no compromise with the quality as a deformed and immature material will never yield good result. The material collected must be of equal size, disease-free, without insect damage and any deformity. The flower selected should just have entered maturity and must be in full vigour. Irrigate the flower bed a night prior to giving it a cutting and if required, wash it with a soft spray of water to rid it of any dust. The cutting is done in the morning on a sunny day after the dew has dried. Collect more material than you require making up for any loss of material at a later stage.

It is also important to know the right stage for taking the cutting. Some plants are left for drying in the garden under natural conditions. Roses, Daisies and Delphiniums are cut when the flower is about to open while Chrysanthemums and Celosia are cut at half and full bloom stages. Hints have been mentioned in the corresponding page of the flower in this regard in Chapter 6.

Types of Drying

The flowers are dried with a specialized technique to remove moisture so that they are able to retain their form and colour. The dehydration drastically reduces chemical changes and also checks micro-organism growth. Plants also undergo many changes, viz., the stem generally becomes infirm after drying and is supported by supporting material. Following are some commonly practiced drying methods which can be put into effective use in homes.

Air-Drying

It is a common, inexpensive and easy method for drying and is best suited for small flowers growing in clusters. The flower with its shoot is kept in an open basket in the cupboard well-aerated away from sunlight and in a warm, dry place for 2-3 weeks or more. This technique is used for drying the flowers that do not wilt readily such as Acroclinium, Baby's Breath, Bachelor's Button, Bells of Ireland, Cockscomb, Globe Amarnath, Larkspur, Statice, and Straw flowers.

Hang-Drying

Select a healthy flower with a long shoot. Remove the leaves of the lower portion of the shoot and make bunches, tying them with a loose string. Keep them in a dark, dry, warm and well-aerated place till the moisture completely evaporates and when touched the shoot produces a rustling sound. A good air circulation helps to carry away the moisture while ventilation with outside air will flush away the released moisture.

Poppy, Sweet William and Pink preserve their colour when dried in an upright position. A few plants need to be dried by submerging them 2-3 cm in water in a dark room till the water in the container evaporates. Flowers with thin soft stems are dried in trays.

Press-Drying

Pressing of flowers in text books and then keeping them under boxes is an activity most of us have undertaken during childhood. To preserve flowers by press-drying method, take a fresh flower (along with leaves, if required) and place it gently between newspapers, blotting paper or pages of a book taking care that no part is crushed or damaged. Arrange the flowers in such a way that they do not touch each other placing corrugated pieces of paper over and below the flower to allow the moisture to escape freely. Thereafter, press the article enfolding the flowers with a heavy weight. The flowers are kept for 2-3 weeks and checked once a week to see that they are free from fungus. Wet blooms should not be pressed, as they develop a mould. Wax paper is used for pressing delicate flowers. Pressing of the flower for a longer duration makes it stronger. Candytuft, Chrysanthemum, Larkspur, Pansy and Verbena can be dried by this method.

Embedding

In this method, the flower is buried into a mixture of very fine, not very light, desiccant (moisture absorber) about 0.02-0.2 mm, so that it draws moisture from the flower. This method is used to ensure that the petals do not crumble or shrink and colour is retained. Dry weather conditions are favourable for its effectiveness.

Silica gel crystal is a little expensive but is commonly used being reusable and time saving. The crystals are blue in colour but after absorbing moisture they turn pink. Drying the crystals in full sunlight for a complete day can recharge them for reuse.

Borax powder is   light in weight

and can be used for drying delicate flowers either in pure form or with a mixture of corn meal to make it heavy. When borax is used, the flower takes 3-9 days to dry.

White sand is also a popular drying agent. Take the required quantity of sand in a container and clean it with a common detergent and wash in excess of water till organic salts and materials are eliminated and the water is clear. Gently spread it on a sheet of newspaper and dry it in sunlight.

Methodology: Choose the flower which is to be dried and cut the stem about 2-3 cm below the flower bud. Take a steel wire, 2 mm thin (20-22 gauge florists' wire) and 10-12 inches long, and adjust its length according to the requirement. Make a 2-3 cm long hook, which can be slipped into the bud. Now pass the free end of the wire into the centre of the flower bud and pull it gently so that the hook gets fixed in the bud. Hold the long end just below the flower bud where the wire has come out of it. The wire is now coiled so that it can settle in the drying air-tight container along with the flower.

Spread a layer of silica gel at the bottom of the container and place the flower on it. Lift the flower and hold it slightly above the layer. Pour a small quantity of the desiccant from all angles till the desiccant establishes complete contact with each part of the flower and finally bury it in the container so that the original shape is maintained. Close and seal the container to make it air-tight and keep it in a cool and dark place.

The silica crystals will turn pink after 2-3 days and it is time to withdraw the flowers as keeping them for a longer period will make them brittle. Open the container and remove the top layers of the desiccant with the help of a spoon. Slowly withdraw the flower from upside down. Then tap it gently or give a blow to remove the desiccant. A fine hairbrush proves handy for removing the fine desiccant held up in some locked areas. Hold the steel wire near the flower bud and straighten it; wrap the floral tape on the steel wire and attach leaves. The flower is now ready for display.

Other Methods

There are other methods for drying but they are not commonly used in home as they need special equipments, proper training, correct methodology and technical know-how. Cryo-drying is a method in which the flowers are dried at sub-zero conditions up to 75 degree Celsius. Oven drying yields excellent results if the plants are kept at a controlled defined temperature and duration. Microwave drying is the fastest way of drying as heat is generated by electronically disturbing water molecules in the flowers. The heat induces evaporation. The methodology is simple: the flowers embedded in a desiccant are placed in a non-metallic container and kept in the microwave oven for a set time. The time varies from flower to flower. Thereafter, the container is kept at ambient temperature so that the moisture is evaporated and the flowers are completely dried. This method is most suited for short flowers which can easily fit in the microwave.

Dry Arrangement

The principle and steps used for dry arrangement are the same as that applied for fresh arrangement, the only difference being in the material used. A great variety of dried materials, e.g. wood rose, wood berries, dried twigs, bulrushes, poppy heads, ferns, husk, etc. are suitable for these arrangements. The suitable containers for these arrangements are large pottery bowls, jugs, trays, metal containers, baskets, boxes and drift wood as base. Dry materials may be painted, varnished or treated to give them colour and shine.

Among the seasonal flowers which are commonly used in dry decoration are Acroclinum, Bells of Ireland, Gomphrena, Helichrysum, Nigella and Statice.

Other Materials for Dry Arrangement

Seeds, seedpods, fruits, wood roses, wood berries, cones, poppy heads, fir, beans, stalks of wheat, corn or oat, etc. are used in parallel to dried flowers. A root drift wood, birch bark or a small dead tree can add texture interest in the arrangement. The arrangement can be painted in golden, silver or brown to make it eye-catching. Ideal containers are large or small baskets, antique boxes, copper vessels, and pottery jugs. In dry arrangements, China or glass vases are not a good choice. A few precious things like grapes of green jade and rose quartz enhance the artistic value whenever they are used.

Useful Tips:

▶ Select bright coloured, disease-free and undamaged flowers.

▶ Flowers in blue, pink and purple fade quickly while orange and yellow retain their colour.

▶ Maintain the original shape of the flower while embedding it in the desiccant.

▶ Post-drying care of dry flowers is essential.

If dried flowers lose their moisture and become brittle, they should be kept in dry and dust-free containers containing silica gel.

▶ Protect the dried flowers from direct sunlight to prevent fading of their colours.

▶ Regularly clear the dust using a soft brush and a hair dryer at slow speed.

▶ Protect them from insect attack that can cause much damage.

Diseases, Pests and their Control

The good health of a plant is also the wealth of the gardener. A disease-free garden with healthy flowers looks beautiful while one with damaged and crumbled vegetation is an eyesore. A gardener has to look after the well being of plants, adopt some pest control measures and check the spread of diseases and pests. These efforts will always give encouraging results and save you from the trouble of pests and diseases.

To keep plants in a healthy state they need a clean environment and balanced nutrients. The quality of the soil is important and it needs to be well-maintained. The organic materials improve the health of the plant when applied in appropriate quantity. If these are applied in an arbitrary fashion, bacteria and fungi flourish and give rise to numerous diseases. Water is essential for survival but over-watering may develop physiological disorder and accelerate growth of harmful micro-organisms. A well-drained soil is the pre-requisite of most of the flora. A physiological disorder in a plant leads to diseases while a pest causes external and physical damage to the plant.

Causes of Diseases

Diseases in plants are caused either by parasitic or non-parasitic organisms. Fungi, bacteria, and viruses act as chief parasites in plants as they themselves are not capable of producing their own food and depend on the plant for the same. The organism, which comes under attack, is the host and that which feeds on it is known as the parasite. Non-parasite diseases are caused due to unfavourable growing conditions and imbalanced nutrition. Lack of nutrients also causes deficiency diseases in plants, which are identified from their respective symptoms.

Viruses are non-living ultra-microscopic entities that come to live and multiply within the plant system. However, their effect and causes are noticed as mottling, curling and discolouring of leaves. There is no cure for the diseases caused, but using insecticides can check the spread of their insect vectors (carriers which spread the disease). The affected plants cannot be cured and should be destroyed as soon as symptoms are noticed.

Fungi are microscopic and can live within the tissues of the plant's surface showing external symptoms. Fungi propagate through spores of varied forms, which spread through insects, air and water and make brown or black spots while mildew diseases form powdery substance on the plants.

Bacteria are unicellular micro-organisms that affect the tissue cells of plants and cause their decomposition, eventually resulting in the collapse of the plant.

Pre-emptive Control

A remedial measure is better than the damage caused thereafter. Given below are a few general control measures that will help in checking pests and diseases in plants.

▶ Sterilize the soil prior to sowing by exposing the soil to the sun for 12-15 days or by using chemicals like Bavistan/Caftaf.

▶ Remove the hosts or the carrier of diseases and pests.

▶ In case of any disease immediately detach the infected part of the plant. If the attack is severe and spread is on the entire plant, uproot and destroy it.

▶ Manually kill the insects if the area is small and the attack is limited.

▶ Grow flowers in the recommended condition of soil texture, drainage, and sunlight to avoid physiological diseases.

Chemical Remedies

Once a disease infects the flowering plants, the only remedy is to use chemical pesticides. However, the chemicals cannot fully repair the damage already caused by diseases.

Handling of Pesticides and other Chemicals

▶ Store only a few select insecticides and fungicides as these will cover the entire range unless some specific ones are needed.

▶ Take note of the 'Expiry Date' before purchase. Read the instructions carefully and implement them accordingly. As flowering plants are very sensitive, ensure that the mixture is made strictly as per the suggested dilution ratio by an expert because a slight over-dose can prove to be harmful and under-dose will be ineffective.

▶ All pesticides are poisonous in nature. Mark it distinctly with red with the words '**POISON**' and keep it away from the reach of children. If possible make available the recommended antidote.

▶ Protect yourself from harmful effect of chemicals by covering your body, especially the face and wound, if any, during the application. Wash your hands and face properly after the spray. Safety of the operating persons is also the concern of the user.

▶ Spraying should preferably be done in the evening on a dry day. A rainy day will wash the contents of the spray. Best results are obtained when spray and dusting are done on a dry day, before fog and dew formation.

▶ The wind factor should be considered prior to spraying. A calm day should be preferred as breeze may carry the contents to the adjoining areas and the infected crop will be devoid of the treatment.

▶ Use a spray pump that can develop high pressure mist so as to cover the entire foliage. A low-pressure spray pump will not be able to give coverage and cause the chemical to drip

from the leaves resulting in waste of chemicals.

◗ Once the spraying is done, clean the container in which the mixture was prepared and store it in a secure place. The packing of the chemicals should be disposed off properly.

◗ Use chemicals from reputed companies only. Some of the commonly used chemicals are as follows:

Fungicides – Baviston, Captaf and Dithane M-45.

Insecticides – 1. For sucking insects like aphids, scales, etc. Chlorpyrifos 20% (Radar), Monocrotophos and Dimethoate 30 % (Rogar) are used.

2. For chewing insects like caterpillars, beetles, etc. Malathon 50% (Tagthion), Dichlorvos 76% (Nuvan) and Endosulfan are used.

Useful Tips:

◗ In poor soil, aeration retards nutrients intake.

◗ Drying of flower leaves results due to water shortage.

◗ Dehydration takes place first in older parts and then in younger flowers.

◗ Humid conditions encourage attack of pests and diseases.

◗ Diseases and pests form a typical pattern on the leaves and if there is no pattern it is due to over-watering.

Pests

Pest	Damage	Control	Affected Plants
Ant Ants are tiny social insects living in colonies consisting of workers, males and queens. They form nests in cracks of walls, floors and roofs of buildings.	Makes tunnels in the ground and makes unsightly mounds especially in the lawn.	Spread turmeric powder on the ants' holes and also around the plants. 2% of Chlorphyiphos powder can also be spread around the infected area.	Gardens, Lawns, Bulbs of Dahlia, Aster.
Aphid (Tela) A tiny sucker insect having blue, black or green colour. It secretes a sticky substance on which black mould is produced. It sucks the sap and reduces the vigour of the tender growing points.	Feeds on the sap of the leaves, buds and flowers. It attacks the plant at seed formation stage.	Spray Roger 0.3%, 3 ml in one litre of water; and 2 ml Malathion in one litre of water.	Antirrhium, Chrysanthemum, Cineraria, Dianthus, Laskpur, Lupin, Poppy, Petunia, Sweet Pea, Rose, Stock.
Blister Beetle The prominent large beetle has alternate orange and black bands on the body.	Feeds on vegetative parts and floral parts resulting in non-formation of flowers.	Physical picking and killing of pests; Dusting of Malathion 5% on leaves and Nuvacron 0.05%, 5 ml in one litre of water.	Aster, Celosia, Chrysanthemum, Gompherena, Marigold, Petunia, Rose.
Caterpillars Hairy, slender long body bearing greenish colour.	Eats foliage of the plants and attacks the plants at seed formation stage.	Dusting of Malathion 5% on leaves; Endosulfan 35 EC in one ml per litre of water.	Aster, Antirrhium, Celosia, Dahlia, Hollyhock.

Pest	Damage	Control	Affected Plants
Earthworm It has a long segmented body. It is formed in the wet soils of lawns and gardens rich in organic matter.	Thin population is beneficial by improving drainage and aeration.	Dense population spoils the grass by making worm cast which gives an ugly look to the garden grass. Solution of hydrate lime; Potassium permagnate crystals, dilute 20-30 grams in 5 litres of water.	Garden Grass.
Mite A microscopic small e i g h t - l e g g e d arthropod having a s p i d e r - l i k e appearance. It is brown and red in colour.	Feeds on the sap of the plant making it dry. It hides under the leaves.	Remove the affected part of the plant. It does not like wet conditions so it is advisable to sprinkle water regularly. Sprinkle Roger @ 2 ml in one litre of water.	C a r n a t i o n , Chrysanthemum, Gerbera, Roses, Hibiscus.
Mealy Bug It is white in colour with wool-like hairs.	Sucks sap and feeds on tender parts of the plants just like aphid. Males are winged while the female is wingless.	Expose the soil to sun. Dust Lindane 2% around the plant; Malathion 5 ml in 1 litre of water; Nuvacron 3 ml in one litre of water; Roger 2 ml in one litre of water.	Phlox, Hibiscus, Croton.
Scale Insects An adult bears a brownish hard shell.	They are found in clusters on stems and under leaves. They feed on the sap of the plant resulting in drying up of the plant.	Monocrotophos 0.5% @ 5 ml in one litre of water.	Phlox, Rose, Fern, Cacti.

Pest	Damage	Control	Affected Plants
Nematodes Microscopic worm found in soil.	Affect root growth, forming root knots.	It is difficult to eliminate the Nematodes form the affected soils. Rotate the flowering beds by growing marigol. Sprinkle Nemagon thoroughly on the soil followed by flood irrigation.	Chrysanthemum, Dahlia, Rose, Tuberose.
Sparrow A common bird, the female is greyish-brown above and ash-white below. The male is dark above with prominent white cheeks.	It feeds on the young seedlings to eat the seeds in root formation.	Keep twigs of dry branches on the young seedlings and cover them with cloth or polythene sheet.	Sweet Pea, Sweet Alyssum.
Thrips These are tiny white insects with slender body and have black wings.	Injures the tissue to make it hollow and sucks the sap causing discolouring of the flowers.	Spray of Malathon, 2 ml in one litre water is quite effective.	Carnation, Chrysanthemum, Cineraria, Dahlia, Gerbera, Nasturtium, Phlox, Rose, Lilies, Tube Rose.
Termite/White Ant Termites make small earthen mounds that are visible above the ground. On opening, greyish-white wingless insects are seen moving inside the mound.	Cuts the stem and roots of the plants. It also feeds on old wood.	Keep the soil wet to discourage the establishment of pest. Use mature manure or compost as immature FYM in the soil lures their housing. Treat the ground with chlorphyiphos before rainy seasons set in.	Aster, Chrysanthemum, Rose, woody parts of the plant.
Squirrels It is a small, four-legged mammal with long furry tail which lives mainly on trees.	Eat seedlings.	Spread few grains of Thimet around the seedlings.	Generally all plants.

Diseases

Disease	Symptoms	Control	Plants Affected
Damping Off	It is a fungal disease that causes wilting of young seedlings by attacking the lower portion of the plant – the stem and the root system.	Sterilization of the soil as discussed in the previous chapter; Ensure good drainage and do not over-water the seedlings; Captaf spray of 4-5 ml in one litre of water; Seed treatment with Captaf/Thiram.	All plants.
Die Back	Fungal attack on the root system of the plant.	Prune the infected part and apply copper sulphate paste on the cut; Removal of the entire plant if the attack is severe.	Rose.
Blight	Fungus forms dark brown/black concentric spots on the lower side of the foliage.	Use Dithane M-45, 0.2%, 2 ml in one litre of water for 100 sq. ft. area; Spray Captan 0.2%, 2 ml in 1 litre of water for 100 sq. ft. area.	Dahlia.
Leaf Spots	Produce small dark brown irregular spots and concentric circles caused by fungal or bacterial infection. The fruiting bodies are responsible for the fall of leaves.	Burn the infected leaves; Use Dithane M-45, 0.2%, 2 ml in one litre of water for 100 sq. ft. area.	Zinnia, Calendula, Hollyhock.
Powdery Mildew	Greyish white patches with white powdery growth on the surface of the leaves.	Do not over-crowd and over-water the planting; Dust sulphur powder every fortnight; Use Karathane 0.5%, 5 grams per 10 litre of water.	Carnation, Alyssum, Antirrhium, Balsam, Chrysanthemum, Cineraria, Dahlia, Delphinum, Phlox, Lupin, Rose.

Monthly Garden Reckoner

JANUARY

- Due to intensive cold the growth of winter annuals slows down but as soon as the days warm up the plants show vigorous growth. The flowering beds need regular hoeing, weeding and irrigation.
- Protection from frost is required for some flowers as indicated in their respective plates.
- Chrysanthemums – remove the dead flowers and the shoot tips of the branches approximately six inches.
- Rose – w.e.f. from November to February, commence planting pencil-thick, 6-8 inches rootstock cuttings of roses in beds for propagation. To raise rootstock for their budding during coming winters, remove the sprouts from the rootstock whenever they appear.
- Bulbs of Amaryllis and Haemanthus can be planted in this month. Bulbs of Tuberose can be dug out and stored at a place away from direct sunlight.
- Lawn – regular mowing, watering and weeding must be done.

FEBRUARY

- Winter annuals are in full bloom. Regular irrigation is required to be done.
- Remove the faded flowers to get continuously long bloom.
- Prepare additional flower beds for summer sowing. The soil beds earmarked must be well dug and weed-free. Later, expose the soil to sun in order to sterilize it for a few days.
- Commence sowing of seeds of summer annuals, e.g. Amaranthus, Gomphrena, Kochia, Portulaca, Helianthus and Zinnia.
- New trees and shrubs for which pits have been prepared can be planted in this month only after severe winter is over.
- Cut off the tops of the Chrysanthemums and plant them in the soil in a shady place for the next season. Thereafter, keep the soil moist.
- Roses – remove the faded/spent flowers so as to prevent seed formation in them.
- Bulbs of Tuberose can be sown in this month.
- Regular weeding, mowing and frequent irrigation is required for lawns. A light application of urea towards the month end is beneficial.

MARCH

- Sowing of summer annuals should be commenced in this month.
- Late winter annuals are still in bloom which should be regularly irrigated. Continuously remove the faded flowers to prolong the bloom. Identify the best plants for 'seed formation' and uproot the unwanted lot. Later, collect the seeds on maturity.
- Empty the flower pots, wash and keep them in sun till they are re-planted.
- Shift the delicate foliage pot-plants away from direct sunlight.

- Maintain the cuttings of Chrysanthemum.
- Bulbs of Spider Lily, Football Lily, Caladium, Tuberose and Zephryanthus can be planted in this month.
- Rose still continues to bloom; maintain the plants by plucking spent flowers and keep them in good condition by regular irrigation and hoeing.
- As the day temperature sores, the grass in the lawn shows vigorous growth which requires regular mowing and irrigation. Weeds also start appearing which should be removed. A light dose of urea is essential.

APRIL

- Uproot all the exhausted flowers except those whose seeds are to be collected.
- The transplantation of summer annuals continues. As the weather gets warm, the summer annuals need regular watering and fortnightly light application of fertilizers.
- The sterilized flower pots are filled with fresh soil mixture for transplantation of summer annuals.
- Sowing of pending bulbs like Foot Lily and Caladium can be completed in this month.
- Once the leaves of Gladiolus are dried, uproot and collect the corms and cormels. Similarly, collect the bulbs of Narcissus and clean and dry them in shade. The dried and dormant bulbs of Gladiolus and Narcissus should be uprooted, dried, treated with a dose of Bavsitin (0.2%) and again allowed to dry. Wrap them in a cotton bag and store in the refrigerator at a temperature of 4°C.
- Maintain the cuttings of Chrysanthemum.
- Continue routine care of roses and removal of spent flower buds.
- The lawn should be regularly watered, mowed and cleared of weeds.

MAY

- Flowering of summer annuals commence. A regular irrigation and light application of fertilizer is required.
- As the temperature soars cover the foliage plants with nets and give deep irrigation.
- Procurement of seeds of rainy/autumn annuals and preparation of their flower bed should be done.
- Pots and plants can be trained to form compact shape as summer heat soars up. Shifting and shuffling of the pots to shady places is advisable.
- Continue to maintain the cuttings of Chrysanthemum.
- Regular care of bulbs is required.
- Continue routine care of roses and removal of spent flower buds.
- The lawn needs regular watering, mowing and removal of weeds.

JUNE

- Pre-monsoon showers in mid or late June gives respite to plants.
- Summer annuals are at peak of flowering and need complete care.
- Seedling sowing of rainy autumn season flowers are ready to be transplanted into flower beds.

It is time to plant the terminal cuttings of Chrysanthemum in the moist sand under the shade after removing the lower leaves and treating the cut portion with 'seradix mixture'. Thereafter, ensure complete care and keep the bed moist.

Bulbs – maintain the existing plants.

Continue routine care of roses and removal of spent flower buds.

The lawns require regular watering, mowing and removal of weeds.

JULY

Blooming of rainy seasonal annuals commence.

Monsoon is in full swing, and the high humidity results in increase of pests and diseases. Spray pesticides as required.

The foliage plants which were shifted indoors can be moved outdoors under shade.

Drain out excess water from the soil beds and pots.

Transplant the established cuttings of Chrysanthemum in beds or pots.

Bulbs need routine care.

The lawn should be mowed very frequently and kept weed-free. Also, it is time to develop fresh lawns. Before establishing a new garden make the patch weed-free. Removing of root of a dominating weed commonly known as 'Motha' is not sufficient. For complete eradication of 'Motha', dig the soil deep to remove the deeply embedded 'black-coloured knots'. An application of 'round-up' 3-4 times in the new area is an effective way to destroy the 'Motha'. A dose of Di-Ammonium phosphate should be preferred to organic manure as the latter yield excessive crop of weeds. Plug small bunches of grass-roots 15-20 cm apart in the soil preferably in the evening hours or on a cloudy day and keep them moist till they turn green and show fresh growth.

Propagation of pending plantation of trees, shrubs and climbers can be completed. Excessive rains increase moisture and warm temperature boosts vegetative growth.

Roses come under the attack of red-scales which should be taken care of.

AUGUST

The rainy season annuals are in full bloom.

All plants show vigorous growth and if proper weeding and timely care is not rendered the garden gives a jungle look.

Take care for proper drainage in the garden from monsoon wet. Take all precautions as discussed in the previous month to prevent plants from rainy weather.

Rainy season is conducive to the growth of many diseases, parasites and pests. In general, spray Monocrotophos insecticide to check insects and Bavistin to prevent fungal diseases.

Pruning and multiplication of over-growing pot plants can be done by division, and transplanting them into fresh pots.

- Trees and shrubs grow vigorously during this month which should be trained and pruned to keep them in shape.
- Chrysanthemum – in small flowered varieties, pinching is done to stop terminal growth and induce secondary branches while large varieties are trained to bear single flower. A very weak dose of liquid manure is beneficial.
- Rose – regular watering and hoeing should be done.
- Bulbs – routine care is essential.
- Lawn – keep the lawn weed-free and mow the grass 2-3 times a week to maintain carpet-like look. A light dose of urea can be applied in weak growth areas.

SEPTEMBER

- Apply manure and prepare the soil beds according to the requirement of the plant. Refer to the propagation notes adjoining the respective flower illustrations. Commence seed sowing of winter annuals towards the end of the month.
- Young and small plants, which need support, can be staked and supported.
- Chrysanthemums require regular pinching and training. Staking should be done with the help of wooden sticks.
- Double Dahlia – plant the sprouted tubers/bulbs in the soil.
- Bulbs – stop irrigating the summer bulbs once they are dry leaves. Later uproot them after 5-7 days and treat them with Bavistin 0.2% for 15-20 minutes and then store them in a cool place.
- Gladiolus and Nargis can be planted at a week's interval.
- Roses – suckers from the rootstocks of roses should be cut off as soon as they appear.
- Lawn – keep the lawn weed-free and mow the grass 2-3 times a week. Give a light application of urea.

OCTOBER

- Commence transplantation of winter annuals seedlings.
- Holly hock and Sweet Pea are sown directly in the soil and few weeks in advance to have a synchronized effect as they take comparatively longer time to bloom.
- Rooted Double Dahlia cutting should be potted or planted in beds.
- Chrysanthemum commences flowering. The faded flowers should be removed as the blooming gets over.
- Bulbs – planting of Gladiolus corms can be continued in well-prepared soil beds. Bulbs of Chinchirinchi, Lily, Iris (yellow), Iris, Oxalis Pink, Ranuculus, Gladiolus, Narcissus (Nargis) and Freesia can also be planted. Remaining summer, Bulbs can be uprooted once they shed their leaves and stored as described above in September operations.
- Prune roses upto the height 30-40 cm from the ground level in the first week of October and apply well-rotten FYM along with fertilizer. A teaspoon of themit or phorate is applied per plant with first irrigation to control rose-scale and other insect pests.
- Lawn – as the night gets cooler the growth slows down and the green lustre of grass starts losing.
- Mowing once a week and alternatively irrigation maintains the carpet-like effect.

NOVEMBER

- Pending transplantation of winter flowers must be completed.
- Chrysanthemum is in full bloom and requires complete care. Remove the faded flowers regularly.
- Roses – a dose of fertilizer should be given as required and weeding should be done regularly.
- Regularly remove the suckers. Budding of rose root stock can be done.
- Bulbs – regular watering and hoeing should continue for the bulbs sown in the previous month.
- Lawn – mowing of grass should be done sometime around noon when it is free of dew.

DECEMBER

- In this month of winter the temperature drops, the day-length shortens and the sky remains overcast. A light spray of water in the evening and cover during night render protection from the cold which damages the young seedlings. Frost control is important and is done by covering the plants with nets, plastic sheets, and newspapers during the night. Secure firmly and strengthen the protection material to avoid any damage due to its collapse. Sticks of 'sarkanda' at an oblique angle can be dug in the soil giving protection from the north while allowing sunlight from the south.
- Cold temperature retards the growth of the young seedling and a light application of urea is beneficial.
- Short spells of rain at the end of the month or early next month gives relief to the plants.
- Adequate quantity of farmyard manure should be applied to trees, shrubs, climbers and other foliage plants.
- Flower pots should be removed to areas with full sunlight during day and moved indoor during night or covered from frost during night.
- Chrysanthemum – the bloom is almost over. The plants which are considered for multiplication, should be cut 4-5 cm above the ground.
- Roses – application of a dose of fungicide and pesticide is advisable.
- Bulbs – carry out routine care.
- Lawn – follow routine maintenance activities. Regular watering keeps check on the fall of temperature to a great extent.

Glossary

Aeration: Loosening of soil to allow free passage of air and exposing it to chemical action of air by adding inorganic matter or by mechanical methods.

Annuals: The plants that grow from seed, flower, set seed and complete their lifecycle in the same season. In other words, which complete their lifecycle in one year.

Biennial: The plants that are sown grow, develop leaves in the first year and flower, set seed and die in the second year. In other words, those plants that complete their lifecycle in two years.

Bedding plants: Hardy and half-hardy plants that are grown for display.

Bleeding: The loss of sap after cutting the tissue of the plant.

Border: Long, narrow beds along the pavements, fences, trees and shrub plantations.

Broadcast: Spreading of seeds or fertilizers on the top of the soil rather than inside the soil to have even distribution.

Colours:

    Warm colours – Colours composed of yellow & red.

    Cool colours – Colours formed by blue and green colours.

    Primary colours – These are red, blue and yellow from which all other colours are formed.

    Secondary colours – These are green, orange and violet and colours produced by mixing equal proportions of primary colours.

    Tertiary colours – Colours made by mixing primary and secondary colours, e.g. red-orange.

Corms: It is an underground storage part of the plant in compressed form.

Crocks: Broken piece of earthenware (pot).

Damping off: It is caused by fungal disease in which the rotting of seedlings takes place at the surface of the soil.

Disbudding: It is the process of removing unwanted buds from the stem or terminal of a flowering shoot.

Drip line: It is the area directly under the shadow of the plant.

Deciduous trees: Trees that lose their leaves in winters.

Flower types:

    Single flower: Flowers having a single layer of petals.

    Semi-double flower: Flowers having semi-double layer of petals.

    Double flower: Flowers having double layer of petals.

F-1 Hybrid: Seeds produced by controlled pollination of two pure lines.

Free flowering: Flowers which bloom profusely.

Flower duration: Duration from the beginning to the end of flowering.

Focal area: An area in the garden which is rich in design, flora and draws the maximum attention.

Germination: Development of seed into a plant. It is the first stage in the lifecycle of the plant.

Ground cover: Ornamental flowers providing dense cover and requiring minimum care that are generally used to cover the soil between trees and shrubs.

Hardening: Conditioning of plants to withstand transplanting shock.

Hardy plants: These are plants that can survive outdoors throughout the year.

Half-hardy plants: The plants that are only grown in summers as they show resistance to frost.

Harmony: A blending of design in such a way that all components give the effect of a whole.

Heading back: Removing of tips of the shoot so as to induce growth in lateral shoots.

Herbaceous: Plants that do not form persistent woody stem.

Inorganic: Chemicals that do not contain carbon.

Leaching: Drifting away of nutrients from the site of plantation due to excessive watering.

Length of day:

Short day plants: Flowering takes place when the day length is of short day or long nights. The plant remains vegetative in days longer than critical day length.

Long day plant: Flowering takes place when the day length is of long day or short nights. The plant remains vegetative in days shorter than critical day length – a dark period not longer than seven hours.

Day neutral plants: Flowering is independent of day length.

Modified stems: The stems which have adapted to the hereditary needs of the plant.

Mother stock: It is the parent stock from which cuttings are taken.

Mulch: A material to cover the soil with a purpose to prevent weed growth, drying of soil and medium to suddenly check the climatic effects.

Node: A point of intersection on the stem of a leaf or leaves.

OP: Open Pollinated.

Osmosis: It is the process by which molecules pass through a membrane from high osmotic pressure to low osmotic pressure.

Partial shade: An eastern or western exposure of the sunlight to the plant, which is screened from afternoon sun.

Perennial: The plants that complete their lifecycle in three years.

Ph-value: It denotes the acidity or alkalinity of the soil. Neutral value is 7 on the 1-14 scale; below 7 is considered acidic and above 7 alkaline.

Photosynthesis: Manufacture of food (sugar) by the leaves in the presence of sunlight, with the help of carbon dioxide and water. The green colour in plant is due to the presence of a pigment called chlorophyll.

Pinching: Removal of shoot terminal to induce lateral branching.

Rockery/Rock garden: It is an integrated feature of a garden whose size should be proportionate to the garden area. It depicts a mountain slope consisting of stones and boulders of different size and composition. It is the space between layers of stones in mud or space between rocks where plants are sown.

Rooting hormone: It is a chemical to stimulate root growth which is applied at the basal portion of the cutting.

Sunlight:

Full: When sunlight is available to the plant for a period of 8-10 hours in a day.

Partial: It is the availability of sunlight during the morning & evening hours and shade during noon or less than 4 hours or diffused sunlight under shade or cover.

Scion: The shoot of a plant that is cut for grafting and united with the root-stock.

Seed: A reproductive body formed by the plant.

Seedling: A young plant grown after germination of plant.

Shoot: The part that grows from the ground when a plant starts to grow and a new part that grows on plants or trees.

Stem: The main long tick part of a plant above the ground from which leaves or flowers grow.

Soil Types:

Light/Sandy: Soil having more sand and silt and whose grains are felt when touched.

Medium/Loamy: A fertile soil containing rich minerals, humus & with balanced contents of sand, silt and clay. It is the best soil among the three. The texture of soil is between light/sandy & heavy/clayey.

Heavy/Clayey: It is the soil that contains more clay contents and sticks to hands when touched.

Top dressing: Adding or replacing of 2-3 inches of top soil layer with fresh rich soil so as to rejuvenate the soil.

Top soil: The top layer of soil with abundant organic matter.

Vegetative growth: No production of flowers but only of leaves, stems and roots.

Vascular diseases: The disease which penetrates the vascular tissues of the plant.

Wild flower: Naturally growing flowers that are usually not domesticated and rise every year under favourable conditions.

Floricultural Periodicals

Floricultural Today (monthly)
T-30, Ist Floor, Khirki Ext., Malviya Nagar,
New Delhi - 110017.

Indian Horticulture (quarterly)
Business Manager, ICAR,
Krishi Anusandhan Bhavan, Pusa Road,
New Delhi - 110012.

Journal of Ornamental Horticulture (quarterly)
Indian Society of Ornamental Horticulture,
Division of Floriculture and Landscaping, IARI,
New Delhi - 110012.

Progressive Farming (monthly)
Punjab Agricultural University, Ludhiana,
Punjab.

References

Complete Gardening in India
K.S. Gopalaswamiengar
The Hosali Press, Bangalore.

Gardening through Ages
M.S. Randhawa
The Macmillian Co. of India Ltd., Delhi.

Ornamental Horticulture
Vishnu Swarup

Floriculture in India
Dr. G. S. Randhawa & Dr. Amitabha Mukhopadhyay
Allied Publishers, New Delhi.

Plants in Pots
William H. Clark, 1953
Little Brown and Company.

Flowers
Bhanu L. Desai
1970, ICAR, New Delhi.

Propagation of Ornamental Plants
H.S. Grewal

History of Flower Arrangement
Berrall S.J.
Thames and Hudson, London.

Home and Gardens Book of
Flower Arrangement
Betty Massingham
Hamlyn Publishing Group Limited, London.

The Complete Guide to Flower Arrangement
Lalvani
Merehurst Limited, London.

Introduction to Flower Arrangement
Pooleerar, R.
Apple Press, London.

Visual Seeds Gallery

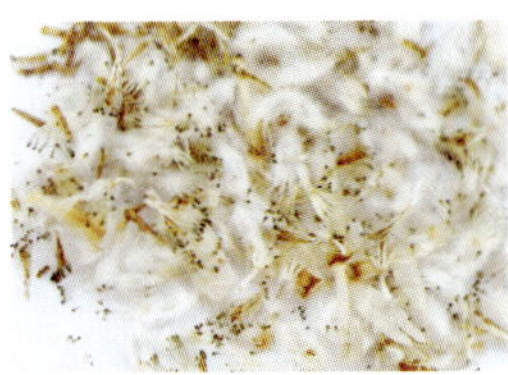

Acroclinum roseum

(Paper Flower)

Althaea rosea

(Holly hock)

Amobium alatum

(Bikni)

Antirrhinum majus

(Dog Flower)

Arctotis stoechadifolia var. grandis

(African Daisy)

Bellis perennis

(English Daisy)

Brassica oleracea

(Kale)

Calendula officinalis

(Pot Marigold)

Callisterphus chinensis

(China Aster)

Centaurea cyanus

(Corn Flower)

Centaurea moschata

(Sweet Sultan)

Cheiranthus cheiri

(Wall Flower)

Chrysanthemum morifolium

(Guldaudi)

Clarikia elegans

(Clarkia)

Coreopsis elegans

(Coreopsis)

Cosmos bipinnatus

(Cosmos Mexican Aster)

Dahlia variabilis

(Dahlia)

Dahlia variabilis

(Dahlia)

Delphinium ajacis

(Larkspur)

Dianthus barbatus

(Sweet William)

Dianthius caryphyllus

(Carnation)

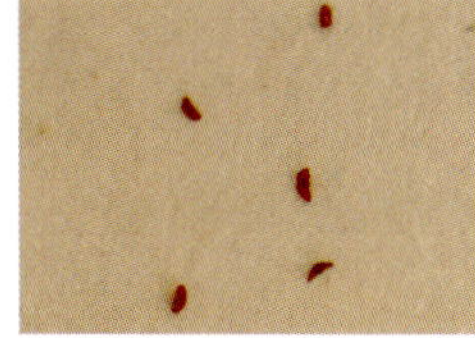

Dianthius chinensis

(Pink)

Dimorphotheca aurantiaca

(African Daisy)

Eschscholzia californica

(California Poppy)

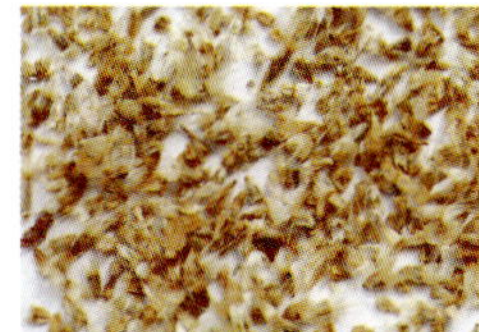

Gaillardia pulchella

(Blanket Flower)

Gamolepsis tagetets

(Matricaria)

Godetia grandiflora

(Satin Flower)

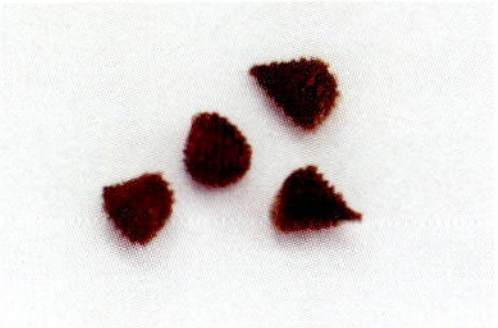

Gypsophila elegans

(Baby's Breath)

Gazania splendens

(Treasure Flower)

Helichrysum bracteatum

(Everlasting Flower)

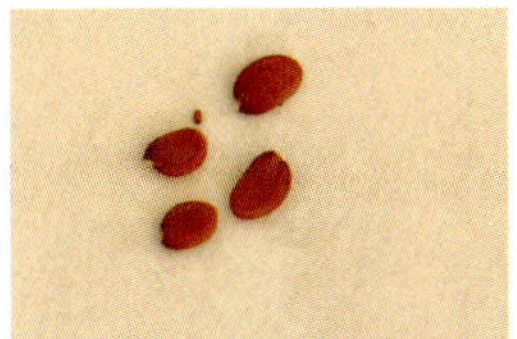

Iberis amara

(Candytuft)

Lathyrus odoratus

(Sweet Pea)

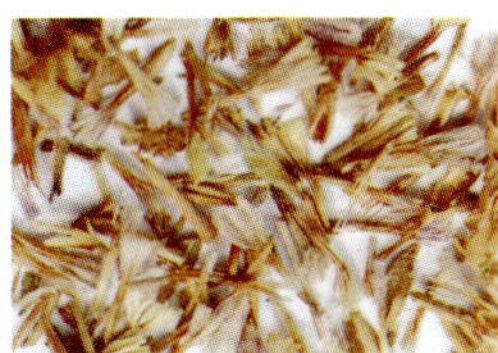

Limonium sinuatum

(Statice)

Linaria maroccana

(Linaria)

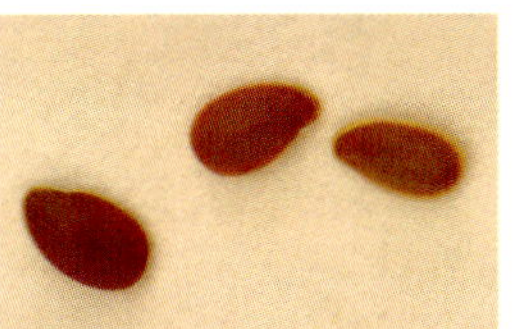

Linum grandiflorum

(Linum)

Lobularia maritima

(Sweet Alyssum)

Lupinus hartwegii

(Lupin)

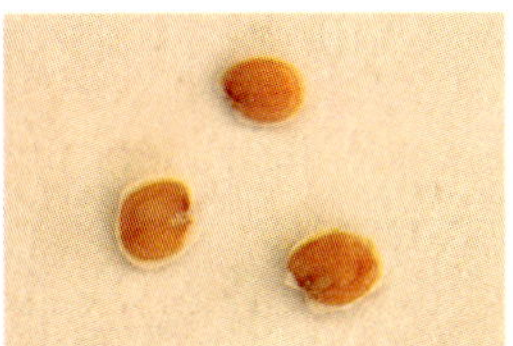

Matthiola incana

(Stock)

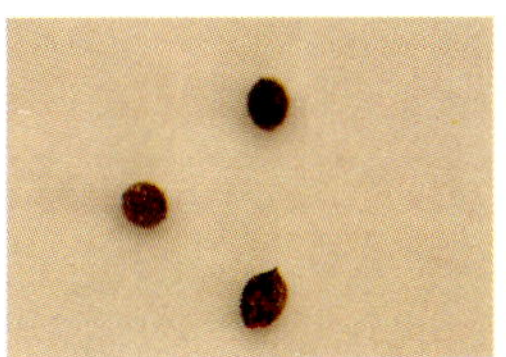

Mesembryanthemum criniflorum

(Ice-Plant)

Mimulus tigrinus

(Monkey Flower)

Molucella laevis

(Bells of Ireland)

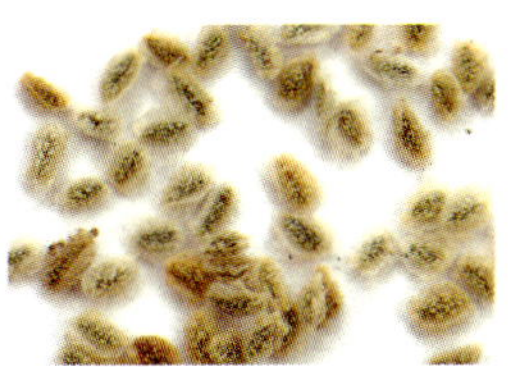

Nemesia strumosa

(Nemesia)

Nigella domascena

(Love-in-a-Mist)

Papaver rhoeas

(Corn Poppy)

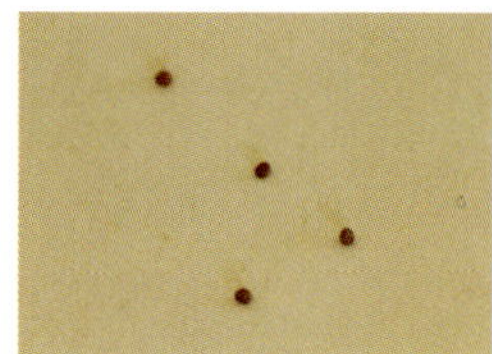

Petunia hybrida

(Petunia)

Phlox drummondii

(Phlox)

Pimpinella monoica

(Lady's Lace)

Salvia splendens

(Scarlet Sage)

Senecio cruentus

(Cineraria)

Tagetes erecta

(African Marigold)

Tagetes patula

(French Marigold)

Tropaeolum majus

(Nasturtium)

Verbena hybrida

(Verbena)

Viola tricolor

(Pansy)

Coreopsis tinctonia

(Coreopsis)

Cosmos sulphureus

(Cosmos)

Helianthus annus

(Sunflower)

Kochia scoparia

(Kochia)

Portulaca grandiflora

(Sun Plant)

Zinnia elegans

(Zinnia)

Celosia argentea var. plumosa

(Celosia)

Celosia argentea var. cristata

(Cockscomb)

Tithonia rotundifolia

(Mexican Sunflower)

Impatiens balsamina

(Balsam Gulmendi)

Garden Notes

Garden Notes

Garden Notes